The heart of prayer

90- days of guided prayer & devotionals
in collaboration with

METRO
COMMUNITY
CHURCH

Edited by:

Shannon McWhorter, Mike Rumsey, Crystal Persons,
Chris Persons, and Mati Barron

·Introduction·

I am so incredibly excited that you are embarking on this prayer journey with us!

I am expectant that God will show up in a powerful way as you dial up the intentionality in your prayer life. I am Pastor Seth Conerly, the lead pastor of Metro Community Church, and it brings me immense joy to introduce this 90-day devotional book on prayer to you.

Over the next 90 days, we will immerse ourselves in the beauty and power of prayer, discovering how it tethers us to Jesus and draws us closer to him. How crazy is it that we, at ANY GIVEN MOMENT, can talk to the God of the universe? CRAZY! It is a transcendent part of the Christian walk that can reshape and redefine every day of our lives if we let it.

Prayer is not a mere religious obligation but a genuine and profound connection with our Heavenly Father. As we engage in this journey, each day's devotional will be penned by different leaders within our church, each bringing a unique perspective and personal touch to the powerful practice of prayer.

Throughout this 90-day prayer focus, you will have the opportunity to engage in different types of prayer, each serving as a valuable facet of our relationship with God. Let's take a moment to understand these various forms and how they can guide our conversations with God over the coming days (and beyond).

1. Intercessory Prayer:

As a church community, we are called to carry one another's burdens, standing in the gap for our brothers and sisters. Intercessory prayer compels us to come alongside others, lifting their needs, concerns, and dreams before the throne of grace. Our heart's desire should be to pray for others with compassion and faith, trusting in God's loving response to our pleas.

2. Petitionary Prayer:

Our Heavenly Father invites us to come to Him with our requests and needs. Petitionary prayer reminds us that we have a God who cares deeply for us and is attentive to the desires of our hearts. As you delve into these devotionals, you will discover the power of asking in faith and aligning your will with His.

3. Adoration and Worship:

Our prayer life should not be limited to asking for things but also rejoicing in who God is. True worship involves adoring Him for His magnificent attributes, His love, and His faithfulness. Throughout this journey, I encourage you to enter into a deeper level of worship through prayer by celebrating and declaring the greatness of our God as you talk to Him.

4. Thanksgiving and Gratitude:

Gratitude is a beautiful expression of the heart. In these devotionals, you will cultivate a spirit of thankfulness, acknowledging God's goodness, mercy, and grace. Gratitude opens our eyes to the countless blessings surrounding us and draws us closer to the giver of all good things.

5. Contemplative Prayer:

Amid life's busyness, finding moments of stillness and silence before God is essential. Contemplative prayer enables us to listen and sense His presence, fostering a deeper communion with our Creator. As you engage in this form of prayer, you will learn to let go of distractions and embrace the peace that comes from being in His presence.

6. Confessional Prayer:

None of us are without faults or mistakes, but we find forgiveness and restoration in God's presence. Confessional prayer allows us to come before our Heavenly Father with humble hearts, seeking His mercy and grace. There is great freedom in confessing our weaknesses and receiving His cleansing love.

7. The Lord's Prayer:

Jesus gifted us with a model prayer (Matthew 6:9-13), encompassing the essence of proper communication with God. Read through Jesus' model prayer and apply its powerful principles in your daily prayer rhythms.

8. Praying with Scripture:

The Word of God is alive and powerful, and incorporating it into our prayers infuses our petitions with divine wisdom and alignment with God's will. As you delve into this form of prayer, you will discover the transformative impact of praying through and with the Scriptures.

Each day, you will be given prayer prompts to guide you through a few minutes of focused prayer.

Do not feel restricted by the times listed; they are simply meant to be a starting point in directing your prayer time. Don't waste this time. Find a place to focus your mind and enter a fully engaged conversation with God. This looks different for everyone. You may be most focused and open to prayer while working out. Maybe you enjoy sitting in a quiet area in your home in the early morning hours with a cup of coffee. If the weather is pleasant outside, you may find peaceful repose walking through God's creation. I could go on and on. Whatever it is for you, do it!

Let's embark on this journey with open hearts and eager spirits! May we be a church defined by its prayerfulness, seeking God's face and will above all else. I pray this devotional book will become a treasured companion, guiding us through these 90 days of prayer and beyond. Together, let us draw nearer to the one who eagerly awaits our heartfelt conversations.

In Christ,

Pastor Seth Conerly
Metro Community Church

Psalm 1:1-6 | Delighting in God's Word
Taylor Conerly | Edwardsville MetroGroup Leader

As we begin our journey through the Psalms, we receive a compelling invitation in Psalm 1:1-6.

These verses lay the groundwork for a blessed and fruitful life, emphasizing the importance of aligning ourselves with God's Word. The psalmist describes a person who walks in the ways of the wicked versus someone who is faithful to delight in the law of the Lord. There is power in immersing ourselves in God's law day and night, regularly reflecting on and absorbing His Word. By allowing it to sink deep into our hearts and minds, we gain deeper insight, wisdom, and understanding.

The tree planted by a flowing stream is a powerful image of a life rooted in God's Word. Similar to how a healthy tree thrives and produces fruit in its proper season, if we take pleasure in God's Word, our walk with Christ will flourish and grow. This doesn't mean we won't face challenges, but it does help give us the strength and patience to endure them.

On the other hand, the life of the wicked is described as chaff (dry husks) blown away by the wind. They lack stability and a firm foundation because they choose not to align their lives with God's truth, which leads to destruction.

These verses provide a clear picture of the joy that comes from living a life deeply rooted & delighting in God's Word. As we make spending time with God through His Word a priority, our lives become like healthy trees, standing firm, producing fruit and bringing honor to God.

Prayer:

Heavenly Father, help us find delight in Your Word and make it a part of our daily lives. Plant us firmly by the streams of Your truth so that we can thrive in every season. Give us discernment in choosing our friends and protect us from the destructive ways of the wicked. May our lives bear fruit that brings honor to You. In Jesus' name, amen.

Facilitated Prayer:

Find a location where you can focus your mind and calm your spirit as you move into a time of prayer. Spend the next few minutes using the P-R-A-Y prompts to enter into a conversation with God. The prompts are to help focus your time of prayer by taking the guesswork out of who and what to pray about each day.

·Day One·

PRAY:

Praise	Take one minute to praise God for giving us His Word, the Bible.
Repent	Take one minute to repent over a time when you were not aligning your life with God's truth.
Ask for Others	Take two minutes to pray for those you know who are struggling with relationships.
Your Needs	Take two minutes to ask God for a life that bears fruit, bringing honor to Him.

Taking Notes:

_____

_____

_____

_____

_____

_____

_____

_____

_____

_____

_____

_____

Psalm 3:1-8
Penny Critcheloe | Vandalia MetroGroup Leader

Me:

"Oh, no! Was that my alarm? NO! I have already hit the snooze button, twice? Yikes! What a way to begin my day! Now I am already in a rush! OK! I've got this! Dress like you are someone special today for the meeting at 8:00am. Ugh, white gym socks will have to do. Oh, where are my dress shoes? This hair! I NEED COFFEE! Why today? I've got to drive really fast today to make it on time! Get out of my way people! I have a meeting!"

God:

"Good morning my child! So glad you slept well! I have a wonderful day full of sunshine planned for you. Freshly bloomed flowers on the corner for your enjoyment! Wait, you seem frustrated this morning. Do you remember that I am here? Do you remember that I go before you and will be with you; I will never leave you nor forsake you? I was hoping to spend a few moments with you before you begin your day. My child, I do enjoy our time so much together. I want you to feel peace, not anxiety over your day. Oh, you are on your way. I will be right here again tomorrow, waiting for our time together, waiting to provide you with peace.."

Psalm 3:2 A Psalm of David, when he fled from his son Absalom.

How often do we hurry off to begin our day, without beginning our day with our Lord?

David felt like he was in the minority. There may have been as many as 10,000 soldiers surrounding him. Not only did David's enemies view life differently, they actively sought to harm him. David could have trusted his army to defeat Absalom; instead, David depended upon God's mercy. Therefore, David was at peace with whatever outcome occurred, knowing that God's great purposes would prevail.

We can overcome fear by trusting God for His protection in our darkest hour. David was not sitting on his throne in a place of power. He was running for his life from his rebellious son, Absalom, and a host of traitors. When circumstances go against us, it is tempting to think that God also is against us; but David reminds us that the opposite is true. When everything seems to go against us, God is still with us and for us.

If circumstances have turned against you, don't blame God – SEEK HIM!

Facilitated Prayer:

Find a location where you can focus your mind and calm your spirit as you move into a time of prayer. Spend the next few minutes using the P-R-A-Y prompts to enter into a conversation with God. The prompts are to help focus your time of prayer by taking the guesswork out of who and what to pray about each day.

PRAY:

Praise	Take one minute to thank God for His trustworthiness to help you face whatever lies ahead.
Repent	Take one minute to readjust your focus and truly seek Him.
Ask for Others	Take two minutes to pray for those that need reassurance of God's purpose, presence, and power in their life.
Your Needs	Take two minutes to give God your fears and place your trust in Him.

Taking Notes:

_____

_____

_____

_____

_____

_____

_____

_____

·Day Three·

Psalm 4:1-8 | Delighting in God's Word
Josh Dickerson | Edwardsville MetroGroup Leader

When you lay your head down to sleep at night, have you ever found yourself wide awake because too many thoughts of fear, stress, or anxiety are dancing around in your head? Have you thought, "What's going to happen, what am I going to do, how can I fix this problem, how can I fix that problem?" The next thing you know, it's early in the morning and you are still unable to sleep!

I have struggled with these thoughts lying in bed in the past and still do on occasion. The way I learned to move past these thoughts is to learn some wisdom from David and start giving these negative thoughts to God; because ultimately, He is the one in control. David tells us in Psalm 4:8, "I will both lie down and sleep in peace, for you alone, Lord, make me live in safety."

We can trust in the Lord no matter what trials have come our way. He has been with us since the beginning and will continue to be with us throughout the rest of our days into eternity.

If you ever find yourself lying awake at night in fear of the day to come, remember, there is nothing in this world that is bigger than Him. Go to Him in prayer and ask God to take away the worries of this day so you might sleep peacefully in His safety.

Facilitated Prayer:

Find a location where you can focus your mind and calm your spirit as you move into a time of prayer. Spend the next few minutes using the P-R-A-Y prompts to enter into a conversation with God. The prompts are to help focus your time of prayer by taking the guesswork out of who and what to pray about each day.

·Day Three·

PRAY:

Praise	Take one minute to thank God for watching over your life.
Repent	Take one minute to reflect on what robs you of a peaceful night's sleep and give it to God.
Ask for Others	Take two minutes to pray for those who need the peace of mind that comes from knowing God.
Your Needs	Take two minutes to hand over to God anything heavy in your life so you can sleep in His safety.

Taking Notes:

_____

_____

_____

_____

_____

_____

_____

_____

_____

_____

_____

Psalm 6:1-10

John Sendejas | Edwardsville MetroGroup Leader

As our kids get older, many times conversations seem to shift towards things they need or want. This is not necessarily a negative or undesirable circumstance because we want our kids to know we are there for them if we can help, as long as the requests are not extravagant or unreasonable.

When they were younger, what they wanted more than almost anything was to be there with you... to watch a TV program, go for a bike ride, get a pizza, or to just sit on your lap.

As Christian adults looking at our relationship with our Heavenly Father, we many times have taken a similar path. Our happiness after receiving Christ was one of excitement and security, knowing that He would always be there and would always listen. As new believers, truth popped off the page as we read each verse. We felt so blessed to know that this most powerful God not only knew us but also that His word emphasized over and over again how much he loves us and will always care for us.

As maturing believers, let's take the time to not just go to God with our requests and wants. Instead let's approach Him like our kids approached us...just wanting to be near us. Their happiness was found in the security and love they felt from us. We should find our joy in the security and love we experience from God.

He will always be there, we just need to go to Him.

Facilitated Prayer:

Find a location where you can focus your mind and calm your spirit as you move into a time of prayer. Spend the next few minutes using the P-R-A-Y prompts to enter into a conversation with God. The prompts are to help focus your time of prayer by taking the guesswork out of who and what to pray about each day.

·Day Four·

PRAY:

Praise	Take one minute to enjoy that God wants you to "sit close" as you pray.
Repent	Take one minute, before you ask God for anything, to simply be near to Him.
Ask for Others	Take two minutes to pray for those who need to know how much God desires to be near them.
Your Needs	Take two minutes to pray for God to reveal His truth when you read His Word.

Taking Notes:

_____

_____

_____

_____

_____

_____

_____

_____

_____

_____

·Day Five·

Psalm 7:10-17
Donna Hagan | Edwardsville MetroGroup Leader

In ages past, a shield was an essential piece of armor when going into battle. It provided the warrior with a personal defensive weapon to deflect and repel arrows, fiery darts, or other deadly projectiles intent on maiming or killing the fighter. The mighty shield was held or strapped in one hand while the other hand engaged in battle against the enemy. The shield, often decorated with colors or symbols to represent its army, not only provided protection during combat, it gave the fighter courage to forge ahead against the enemy for his king or commander.

As Christians, the shield which we lift up and carry is our faith in God Most High. In times of physical trials and spiritual attacks which assault us, we hold tightly to our trust that God is our protector shielding us from harm. He loves us and watches over us. We surrender our doubts and ask God to help us in our struggles. We have faith that God, in his mighty power and wisdom, will shield us from our enemy who is shooting fiery darts at our heart, mind, or body. We believe that God is our righteous judge who will defend us, declare punishment on our enemies, and restore us as He meets our needs.

Then, after we take up our shield and put our struggles or needs in God's hands, we engage in the battle with praise and thanksgiving. It often takes courage to praise and thank God when we haven't yet seen the answer to our prayers or we are still stuck in a difficult situation. Our praise reminds us that God, our King, is in control, and our thanksgiving reaffirms our faith that God will work everything out for our good because we love Him.

Facilitated Prayer:

Find a location where you can focus your mind and calm your spirit as you move into a time of prayer. Spend the next few minutes using the P-R-A-Y prompts to enter into a conversation with God. The prompts are to help focus your time of prayer by taking the guesswork out of who and what to pray about each day.

·Day Five·

PRAY:

Praise	Take one minute to dwell on knowing "God Most High", your source of hope in all circumstances.
Repent	Take one minute to rediscover and repurpose your shield of faith in God Most High.
Ask for Others	Take two minutes to pray for those who need to use their shield in order to advance on enemies in their life.
Your Needs	Take two minutes to utilize your shield of faith as you face what comes today/tomorrow.

Taking Notes:

_____

_____

_____

_____

_____

_____

_____

_____

_____

_____

_____

·Day Six·

Psalm 8:1-9
Brett Barron | Metro Director of Ministry

Psalm 8 is a hymn of praise to the Lord who works through the weak things of the world – namely humanity – to display His power. His activity within creation inspires worship, astonishment, and awe. Yet, He descends to concern Himself most intimately with His most valuable creation – people. The author, King David, both opens and closes this hymn calling upon Yahweh, our Adonai (my Master), acknowledging that God has made a covenant with all who trust in Him so that He becomes ours. The majesty of our God is great beyond words and worthy of our fervent worship and allegiance. Why is God's name so majestic in all the earth? Why is His name above all names and without rival or equal? Because God, the compassionate Creator, is also consistently active in the business of re-creating.

When the glory of our King is in view, our sin-corrupted minds, all too easily, fall into a pattern of focusing too intently on our apparent worthlessness. Our enemies don't only come at us with a sword or spear; more often than not, the weapon wielded is an intrusive thought, a blind spot, or a misguided mindset that brings guilt and shame. We are left feeling undeserving of the grace, mercy, and love the Lord desires to lavish upon us.

Take a moment to prayerfully consider your rightful position established by God from the onset of creation and by the shed blood of Jesus on the cross. Ask the Lord to re-create in you His original design. We have great worth because we bear the stamp of our Creator God. Because God has already declared how valuable we are to Him, we are set free from feelings of unworthiness. Young children trust their parents without reservation, and perhaps that is why they always seem so carefree. As we get older, praising even in the midst of uncertainty and uneasiness becomes more and more difficult to do. Ask Yahweh, your loving Father to re-create in you a childlike faith, removing any barriers to a closer walk with Him.

Facilitated Prayer:

Find a location where you can focus your mind and calm your spirit as you move into a time of prayer. Spend the next few minutes using the P-R-A-Y prompts to enter into a conversation with God. The prompts are to help focus your time of prayer by taking the guesswork out of who and what to pray about each day.

·Day Six·

PRAY:

Praise	Take one minute to think about what God has done to confirm how much you are worth to Him..
Repent	Take one minute to confess anything that is hindering God's ongoing work of re-creation in your life.
Ask for Others	Take two minutes to pray for someone who needs to know or be reminded of how much God loves and values them.
Your Needs	Take two minutes to express a childlike faith that you need God's help to rediscover.

Taking Notes:

_____

_____

_____

_____

_____

_____

_____

_____

_____

_____

Psalm 9:1-10
Leslie Price | Edwardsville MetroGroup Leader

"That's not fair!" If you've ever been a teacher, parent, or grandparent, you know you've heard this exclaimed many times. The child feels as if an injustice has been inflicted upon him or her. Instead of asking a trusted adult for help in understanding and finding a way to work through the struggle, he/she might take matters into their own hands, trying to "get even" with the one who has been mean or treated them unfairly.

As an adult, I have cried out the same words in different life situations. But God's Word reminds me that He will be the Judge. He will judge with justice. I don't need to take things into my own hands. He's got my back!! He promises to be our refuge in times of trouble. I will trust Him to give me wisdom to make the right choices when I'm feeling oppressed, thinking life isn't fair.

I realize a key part of this trust comes when I seek Him in prayer. I need to talk to God and tell Him how I feel. Like a child, when I exclaim "that's not fair", my Heavenly Father gently and patiently reminds me that He loves me and wants the best for my life. He will never forsake me when I seek Him.

When God is faithful to answer my prayers, I must remember to thank Him with all my heart! I never want to take for granted the times God has watched over me, protected me, and given me wisdom in those hard circumstances. Besides thanking Him, it is also important to give God the glory and share with others what He's done for me. I will tell of all of His wonderful deeds and sing praises to the Most High!

Facilitated Prayer:

Find a location where you can focus your mind and calm your spirit as you move into a time of prayer. Spend the next few minutes using the P-R-A-Y prompts to enter into a conversation with God. The prompts are to help focus your time of prayer by taking the guesswork out of who and what to pray about each day.

·Day Seven·

PRAY:

Praise	Take one minute to reflect on how you feel knowing that you can be honest with God.
Repent	Take one minute to repent of playing the role of judge and/or jury.
Ask for Others	Take two minutes to pray for those who have been treated unjustly and need to know God will judge with justice
Your Needs	Knowing that God will judge, take two minutes to celebrate His mercy and grace in your life.

Taking Notes:

_____

_____

_____

_____

_____

_____

_____

_____

_____

_____

•Day Eight•

Psalm 9:11-20
Connie Vaitekunas | Edwardsville MetroGroup Leader

"God, I've got this. I know exactly what I need to do and say." Have you ever said something like this? Well, I've done this more times than I want to share, and I end up totally and utterly exhausted...broken.

No one can help me except Abba, my Father. He hears my cries for help, and He responds with His love and grace. I need His protection and He rescues me every time. That's when I realize just how much He loves me and how powerful He is.

God gives me the gift of hope. I praise Him for that and let His love sink into every fiber of my being. Abba protects me from the evil one and those who try to hurt me.

We can be totally honest with our feelings to the LORD. He already knows how we are feeling, so it's okay to verbally tell Him. He wants us to have that kind of personal relationship with Him, but we must first put our trust in Him and not in the things of this world.

As He lifts us up, we in turn lift up others who are struggling and need God to rescue them. Tell people and show them just how much our God is a loving and merciful God. Sing praises to Him and others will also. We are giving them hope through God and His Son Jesus Christ.

Let God lift your heart so you can help lift someone's heart through His love and faithfulness.

Facilitated Prayer:

Find a location where you can focus your mind and calm your spirit as you move into a time of prayer. Spend the next few minutes using the P-R-A-Y prompts to enter into a conversation with God. The prompts are to help focus your time of prayer by taking the guesswork out of who and what to pray about each day.

·Day Eight·

PRAY:

Praise	Take one minute to praise Him, knowing God (Abba) hears our cries with love & grace.
Repent	Take one minute to be completely honest with God.
Ask for Others	Take two minutes to pray for those who need to see & hear us lifting God up so they can find hope in Him.
Your Needs	Take two minutes to pray about what you specifically need in order to help someone else who's struggling.

Taking Notes:

_____

_____

_____

_____

_____

_____

_____

_____

_____

_____

·Day Nine·

Psalm 13:1-6
Diane Savoca | Prayer Team

My "**TO DO**" list just gets longer and longer. Plus, someone is always asking me to do something: family, neighbors, Metro. Like right now....I am to write a devotional.

I have taken time management seminars and even engaged a coach to help me clarify my priorities and create a plan to reach my goals. But I get distracted and tired and ready for a nap by 10 a.m.

Plus, this world is filled with chaos and pain: illness, anger, violence, abuse, and death. It seems like there is always something to mourn. There is death and pain around each corner.... the phone rings and my heart races....who needs help now?

Fact is, I am majorly blessed as I serve. My grandma used to tell me, "When you focus on the pain, it gets worse." And Dad said, "worry is a waste of time. Just determine what you have control over and DO IT. And what you do not have control over, just give it UP." And Mom said, "Be a giver. Look for ways to bless. "

I have a good foundation...but still wonder, "How long will my life be this roller coaster?"

I pray and pray and ask for clarity. What is it that you want from me Lord? I pray that all of my thoughts, words and deeds will glorify You. So, I do make time to pray. But life is still crazy.

So often I spent too much time feeling sorry for myself, complaining, and losing sleep,such a waste of time and energy. It beats down my faith and Satan is celebrating.

Get behind me Satan, as I celebrate my Lord's love and provisions. Jesus, You have never let me down. There have been many challenges, but You always help me through.

I rejoice knowing we will meet in heaven. Oh, glorious day!

Facilitated Prayer:

Find a location where you can focus your mind and calm your spirit as you move into a time of prayer. Spend the next few minutes using the P-R-A-Y prompts to enter into a conversation with God. The prompts are to help focus your time of prayer by taking the guesswork out of who and what to pray about each day.

·Day Nine·

PRAY:

Praise	Take one minute to thank God for being the source of our strength.
Repent	Take one minute to confess when you have doubted God.
Ask for Others	Take two minutes to pray for those who need freedom from their sin that only God can provide.
Your Needs	Take two minutes to seek the Lord for victory in your life where Satan has had a stronghold.

Taking Notes:

_____

_____

_____

_____

_____

_____

_____

_____

_____

_____

·Day Ten·

Psalm 16:1-11
Rick Marteeny | Edwardsville MetroGroup Leader

Being in the insurance business for over 35 years, I've seen my share of storms. During the most severe storms, we are often told to take shelter. Shelter provides cover and protection against danger (the wind, the lightning, the rain, and the hail). We are safe when we have the appropriate shelter protecting us. In fact, along with air, water, and food, shelter is essential for our very survival as human beings.

King David knew where to turn for shelter. He knew he could trust God for protection from his enemies and from danger. David knew that those who acknowledge their need for the Lord, as he did, see Him as the ultimate source of everything good in their lives. They see God as their security, their strong tower, and their mighty fortress.

God provided protection for David time and again in his life. From his hunting days as a boy, to his battle with Goliath, to being on the run from King Saul....God was constantly protecting David from harm. While David learned to trust God for protection against earthly dangers, he also knew his ultimate security was based on his personal relationship with God for eternity. He knew he would not be "abandoned" by God and allowed to "rot and decay" because his eternal destiny was secure.

We can find that same confidence and joy by turning to God as our refuge and shelter. Today, as you face your own storms, rejoice in the fact you have a mighty shelter protecting you....the God of the universe.

He is with you, He will strengthen you, help you, and hold you up with his mighty right hand (Isaiah 41:10).

Prayer:

Heavenly Father, thank you that I always have you to turn to for protection. Please be with me during the storms of life when I am weak and scared. Help me to see that you are a mighty fortress and always ready to help me in times of trouble. I trust you God. Thank you for being so good and kind to me. In Jesus' name I pray. Amen.

Facilitated Prayer:

Find a location where you can focus your mind and calm your spirit as you move into a time of prayer. Spend the next few minutes using the P-R-A-Y prompts to enter into a conversation with God. The prompts are to help focus your time of prayer by taking the guesswork out of who and what to pray about each day.

·Day Ten·

PRAY:

Praise	Take one minute to praise God for Him being your shelter and protection.
Repent	Take one minute to free yourself from the storms of your life.
Ask for Others	Take two minutes to pray for those who need to find shelter and protection from the dangers in their life.
Your Needs	Take two minutes to seek shelter in God with the current storms in your life.

Taking Notes:

_____

_____

_____

_____

_____

_____

_____

_____

_____

_____

_____

·Day Eleven·

Psalm 17:1-7
Bri Liley | Edwardsville MetroGroup Leader

As outsiders looking in, this passage gives us access and insight into the bold, honest, and vulnerable prayer life of David. Straight from his opening plea, we see how plainly David confesses his longing to see justice brought upon his enemies and how confident he is that God already knows the thoughts and motives behind his request (which are holy and not in vain). Then, bold and blunt as ever, David reminds God that he has stayed close to His will by following His commands, continuing to submit the situation to Him (rather than taking it into his own hands and seeking justice through means of vengeance). It is important to note, though, that David doesn't present God with this list of good deeds so that God, in return, will grant his request. Rather, he is continuing with his plea from verse one, reiterating that his motives and requests are pure and God-honoring. Finally, David ends this section by repeating the truth he knows deep in his soul: that God both hears and answers his prayers.

Intricacies aside, the heart of this scripture passage can be boiled down to just one sentence: **David truly believes that God sees his motives, knows his needs, listens to his prayers, and plans to respond in His own perfect way.**

Throughout this passage, David doesn't attempt to teach anybody how to pray nor does he tout a secret recipe for a successful prayer life. Yet as we reflect on his example, we see that his prayers are bold, honest, and vulnerable because he is praying to the God he has spent decades getting to know, trust, and find comfort. As with so many mature, seasoned Christ-followers, David has given us a fantastic example to follow. Before moving forward with your day, spend some time in prayer as David did. Speak to God with honesty and boldness, praying as if you truly believe He sees your motives, knows your needs, listens to your prayers, and plans to respond in His own perfect way.

Facilitated Prayer:

Find a location where you can focus your mind and calm your spirit as you move into a time of prayer. Spend the next few minutes using the P-R-A-Y prompts to enter into a conversation with God. The prompts are to help focus your time of prayer by taking the guesswork out of who and what to pray about each day.

·Day Eleven·

PRAY:

Praise	Take one minute to dwell and thank God for His attentive presence in your life.
Repent	Take one minute to honestly talk to God about your struggles.
Ask for Others	Take two minutes to approach God boldly on behalf of those you love.
Your Needs	Take two minutes to ask God to see your motives and needs so He can respond in His own perfect way.

Taking Notes:

_____

_____

_____

_____

_____

_____

_____

_____

_____

_____

_____

Psalm 17:8-15
Shannon McWhorter | Edwardsville MetroGroup Leader

"You'll shoot your eye out, Kid."
"Don't stare at the sun."
"Always wear protective eyewear."

Each of those statements refers to protecting one's eyesight.
I have a family history of bad eyesight. I remember my grandmother writing in a very large print with a black felt pen because she couldn't see the fine ink of a ballpoint pen. When I was in high school, my dad had surgery on both of his eyes due to detached retinas. By the time I was in my twenties, I had a severe myopic prescription; yes, I wore coke-bottle glasses. As a result of this family history, I have always tried to protect my eyesight, to guard it.

In Psalm 17, when David asks God to "keep me as the apple of your eye", he is asking God to protect him from his enemies the way one guards one's eyesight. In this prayer, David is quoting Deuteronomy 32 where Moses is retelling the story of how God has led the Israelites for the past 40 years. Moses shares how God found Jacob in the wilderness and "encircled him, cared for him, and kept him as 'the apple of his eye'."

God protected Jacob and so David, familiar with the history of his people, the Israelites, cries out to God to do the same for him—to protect him from his enemies. David is being pursued by his enemies and yet, instead of taking matters into his own hands, he turns to God to protect him, to guard him, and even to take vengeance for his sake, even though his enemies are pursuing him and even seem to be prospering. Whoever or whatever your enemies are today, whether they be other people or your own trauma, emotions or sin, you can call out to God to guard yourself against them.

This psalm closes with another reference to "seeing". David, praising God for His protection from his enemies, knows that his satisfaction comes from seeing God's likeness. Like David, we, too, can only be satisfied when we see His likeness; and His likeness only comes from being in His Word and is stamped upon us by His renewing grace. The only true satisfaction for your soul is found in God.

Facilitated Prayer:

Find a location where you can focus your mind and calm your spirit as you move into a time of prayer. Spend the next few minutes using the P-R-A-Y prompts to enter into a conversation with God. The prompts are to help focus your time of prayer by taking the guesswork out of who and what to pray about each day.

·Day Twelve·

PRAY:

Praise	Take one minute to thank God for His commitment to guard you from harmful circumstances.
Repent	Take one minute to ask forgiveness for taking God's provision and protection for granted.
Ask for Others	Take two minutes to pray for those you know to experience God's provision and protection.
Your Needs	Take two minutes to ask God for His provision and protection in areas of your life where you desperately need Him.

Taking Notes:

_____

_____

_____

_____

_____

_____

_____

_____

_____

_____

·Day Thirteen·

Psalm 18:19-24
Craig Zitta | Edwardsville MetroGroup Leader

In our daily journey, God's presence is in our past, present, and future. The path in front of us can lead us in many different directions. If we choose to follow His path, we will be guided and tested. God loves us regardless of what we did or where we go. He rewards us with undeserving love and grace. We are told he will fight our battles in His time and His ways. When we give battle to God, we need not take it back.

I have followed God through a season that was impossible for me to understand and acknowledge. He guides us through life in a Godly, sometimes unknown, path. God's ways are not our ways. We need only to follow in his footsteps. God knows our innocence.

We are blessed with our amazing ability to follow Him.

Facilitated Prayer:

Find a location where you can focus your mind and calm your spirit as you move into a time of prayer. Spend the next few minutes using the P-R-A-Y prompts to enter into a conversation with God. The prompts are to help focus your time of prayer by taking the guesswork out of who and what to pray about each day.

·Day Thirteen·

PRAY:

Praise	Take one minute to rejoice in how amazing God's presence has been/will be in your past, present, and future.
Repent	Take one minute to recognize a "battle" you have taken up on your own terms, and release it over to God.
Ask for Others	Take two minutes to pray for those who need to know that God's rules and statutes are given with divine wisdom.
Your Needs	Take two minutes to pray that Jesus gives you opportunities to use your God-given ability to follow Him this week.

Taking Notes:

_____

_____

_____

_____

_____

_____

_____

_____

_____

_____

_____

·Day Fourteen·

Psalm 18:25-30
Becky Niebruegge | Edwardsville MetroGroup Leader

Have you ever been in a situation where you couldn't see your way out? That's where David found himself when he wrote this psalm as he was being hunted by the army of King Saul.

God is always with you. God has supplied you with everything you need, and you need to have faith and know His way is the best way. It is all His. He has given you everything that you have. He has your back and will shield you when you take refuge in Him and look to Him as your protector.

He brings the light into the darkness by supplying the oil for your lamps to shine. He moves your troops. He knows what you need and when you need it and He wants you to take refuge and trust in Him. We are tempted to think we can control our lives and do it on our own, but God is the source of all we have. Give glory to God and know He is your protector, your shield. He has proven Himself worthy, so know that He will do it again and again. Find your refuge in God and breathe easy knowing He will walk with you through every storm protecting and shielding you more than you will ever know and getting you out of situations you never thought were possible to escape.

Facilitated Prayer:

Find a location where you can focus your mind and calm your spirit as you move into a time of prayer. Spend the next few minutes using the P-R-A-Y prompts to enter into a conversation with God. The prompts are to help focus your time of prayer by taking the guesswork out of who and what to pray about each day.

·Day Fourteen·

PRAY:

Praise	Take one minute to thank God for helping you navigate life.
Repent	Take one minute to confess times you have patted yourself on the back and have taken credit for your success in life.
Ask for Others	Take two minutes to pray for those who are wandering, in need of a guide to help them navigate their life's journey.
Your Needs	Take two minutes to pray about what lies around the next "bend in the road" in your life. Ask God to be your guide.

Taking Notes:

_____

_____

_____

_____

_____

_____

_____

_____

_____

_____

·Day Fifteen·

Psalm 18:25-30
Leanne Bales | Vandalia MetroGroup Leader

I remember memorizing Psalm 19:14 at church when I was a pre-teen. "Let the words of my mouth and the meditation of my heart be acceptable in Your sight, O Lord, my strength and my Redeemer." I really wanted to please God with my life; I focused on being a kind person and speaking kind words to the people I came in contact with. Growing up in church allowed me to learn about God's law, His perfect love for us, and following His commandments. Obedience to God was important to me.

As I became an adult and lost the innocence of youth, I strayed from the faith of my youth. But I still remembered God's Word and knew through prayer that I could be forgiven of my sins – God would take away my guilt and shame and help guide me back onto the direct path to follow Him and restore my joy.

Praying daily (for me several times a day) is the best way to talk with God. When I study the Bible I ask (pray) for clarity and understanding as I am seeking wisdom and direction.

Would you change the way you live if you knew that every word and thought would first be examined by God?

Facilitated Prayer:

Find a location where you can focus your mind and calm your spirit as you move into a time of prayer. Spend the next few minutes using the P-R-A-Y prompts to enter into a conversation with God. The prompts are to help focus your time of prayer by taking the guesswork out of who and what to pray about each day.

·Day Fifteen·

PRAY:

Praise	Take one minute to praise God for seeds of faith He planted in your past which have blossomed later in life.
Repent	Take one minute to confess when you have viewed God's rules as restrictive rather than protective.
Ask for Others	Take two minutes to pray for those who need to know that God watches, listens, and walks alongside us.
Your Needs	Take two minutes to pray for God's presence as you navigate your week.

Taking Notes:

_____

_____

_____

_____

_____

_____

_____

_____

_____

_____

·Day Sixteen·

Psalm 23:1-6
David Stokes | Vandalia MetroGroup Leader

Having grown up on a farm and choosing farming as my profession, I've been around livestock a great deal of my life. About four years ago I sold my cows to a neighboring farmer. More than a year later I saw him out feeding his cows and I stopped to talk to him. He told me the cows that had been mine would not come up to feed with the rest of the herd. I asked if he called them, and he said that he had not. I yelled "come on girls" in the singing way I always said it. The ones I had sold him lifted their heads and started our way! They knew my voice...just like we read in John 10:27.

A little over ten years ago, I had a spot on my skin that was unusual. It really didn't concern me, but after my wife insisted, I had it examined. I made an appointment with a dermatologist. He took one look at it and said I needed to visit a specialist in St. Louis. He recommended a doctor and in a short time we saw him. Upon examining the spot, the doctor said, "Oh yes, that's cancer...an unusual cancer."

It didn't cause me as much concern as it did my wife. I knew that the Lord is My Shepherd. I had "a peace". I knew His voice. I really didn't have fear. John 10:27 tells us that His sheep know His voice. When I read the Bible, sometimes I listen for His voice. Sometimes I can hear His voice during worship service or the message. Sometimes I hear His voice during small group studies.

I know the Lord is my Shepherd. He will protect me with His rod and guide me with His Shepherd's crook. Because I have trusted Him, I'm assured I will be a part of His household. Forever.

Facilitated Prayer:

Find a location where you can focus your mind and calm your spirit as you move into a time of prayer. Spend the next few minutes using the P-R-A-Y prompts to enter into a conversation with God. The prompts are to help focus your time of prayer by taking the guesswork out of who and what to pray about each day.

·Day Sixteen·

PRAY:

Praise	Take one minute to praise how God as your shepherd takes care of you.
Repent	Take one minute to ask God to redirect you with His rod and staff.
Ask for Others	Take two minutes to pray for those in your life that need to respond to the Shepherd's call.
Your Needs	Take two minutes to ask God to lead you from what you read in Psalm 23.

Taking Notes:

_____

_____

_____

_____

_____

_____

_____

_____

_____

_____

_____

·Day Seventeen·

Do you ever feel inadequate? Do you ever feel like the task that is in front of you is more than you are able to withstand or bear? Sometimes the stress of work, raising kids, family relationships, a health diagnosis, stress of school, or caring for aging parents can make me feel I'm inadequate and that I can't bear any more pressure. There are probably a million more things that you can add to this list that make you feel similarly stressed.

When you read Psalm 24, I hope a peace washes over you, like it does over me. My perspective shifts to a focus on God whom I serve, who is in control of the whole earth and everything in it. I don't have to control anything. I don't have to bear the weight of any of it. I seek and have a relationship with the God of Jacob so I can rest comfortably in His hands, all the while knowing that the One who has all the power and control has it all under control.

As you read verses 7-10, read it as if you are pumping yourself up for battle. It's not a battle you are fighting alone. You have the One Most High, the King of glory, going before you, beside you and behind you.

"Who is the King of Glory? The Lord, strong and mighty; the Lord, invincible in battle." He is your King ready and invincible in any battle. You are adequate and more than enough when you stand with Him, the King of Glory!

God, thank you for your love for me. I am so grateful that I have a relationship with the Lord Most High. The One who controls it all. God let me feel your presence as I walk through this day. Give me your wisdom and courage to face every battle that comes my way today. Help me rest in you today. In Jesus name amen!

Facilitated Prayer:

Find a location where you can focus your mind and calm your spirit as you move into a time of prayer. Spend the next few minutes using the P-R-A-Y prompts to enter into a conversation with God. The prompts are to help focus your time of prayer by taking the guesswork out of who and what to pray about each day.

·Day Seventeen·

PRAY:

Praise	Take one minute to think about the blessing of being in a relationship with the "Lord Most High".
Repent	Take one minute to confess where you are limiting the impact of God's perspective and power.
Ask for Others	Take two minutes to pray for those who need to know the power and presence of God in their life
Your Needs	Take two minutes to lean into God's presence and power in the battles you are currently facing.

Taking Notes:

_____

_____

_____

_____

_____

_____

_____

_____

_____

_____

_____

·Day Eighteen·

Psalm 25:1-11
Stephanie Thomas | Vandalia MetroGroup Leader

I have been struggling with painful events surrounding my father's recent death; I have felt wronged and felt as if I have been treated unfairly. The hurt is very deep. Since the day this struggle began, as I turned to God in prayer, He has answered by sending me clear responses, repeatedly, through my daily devotionals, Bible readings and counsel from my Christian friends and family.

In the beginning, I was so heartbroken over these events that the only prayer I could pray was, "Jesus" again and again. Years ago, I read about a person trying to comfort a friend who had suffered an unimaginable tragedy. There were truly no words that could bring comfort in this moment, so the woman just began praying, "Jesus, Jesus, Jesus" over and over again as she sat with her friend. Slowly she saw her friend's tension release. In that moment there was only a one-word prayer that could provide any level of solace for this woman and that was, "Jesus". That stuck with me. "Jesus" is my "go to" prayer when I am so troubled, hurt, confused or grief stricken that I simply do not have the words to pray.

I sought God's guidance regarding the loss of my father and the hurtful events that followed. During those events, I perceived others had intentionally wronged me. God began to speak clearly to me as I sought His comfort. The passage for this devotional is not different. In Psalm 25:1-11 God provides clear direction and reminders for how to cope with this situation, as well as many other difficulties ALL of us experience:

Psalm 25:2 We are to put our trust in God. He instructs us not to rely on our emotions but instead trust Him. If we allow our "humanness" to guide us, we will be stuck in a place of pain and darkness. Psalm 25:3 God will make sure our enemies will not triumph (Psalm 25:3). If others treat us unfairly, if these individuals are "treacherous without cause," God will deal with them. It isn't our place to do so. We can be at peace, God's got this!

Psalm 25: 4 – 6 God is guiding us and teaching us His way. His way is a path of truth, hope, great mercy and love (not the path of hate, hurt, vindictiveness and bitterness where our human hearts may lead us).

Psalm 25: 7 God is reminding us, we are all sinners. Have I not sinned? Yes, I have. Have I not shown rebellion? Yes. But, God forgives us when we seek Him. He shows us love and goodness. He is guiding us to follow his path and extend mercy to others as He has done for us, even our enemies.

·Day Eighteen·

Psalm 25: 8 – 10 God is instructing us in what is good. We should walk in humility and follow His way. His way is right, loving and faithful.

Psalm 25:11 The final verse ends with forgiveness. I'm confident this is not a coincidence. We must pray for forgiveness when we have wronged others AND forgive those who have wronged us. When we seek God in prayer, He provides comfort, mercy and a path for how to cope with all situations we will experience on earth. This includes those that are difficult to understand and cause us much pain. He will answer our prayers for "surely His goodness and mercy will follow me all the days of my life" Psalm 23:6.

Facilitated Prayer:

Find a location where you can focus your mind and calm your spirit as you move into a time of prayer. Spend the next few minutes using the P-R-A-Y prompts to enter into a conversation with God. The prompts are to help focus your time of prayer by taking the guesswork out of who and what to pray about each day.

As you "P-R-A-Y..."

PRAY:

Praise	Take a minute to praise God for goodness and mercy.
Repent	Take a minute to ask forgiveness for not seeking God in times of crisis.
Ask for Others	Take two minutes to ask God to comfort your loved ones who are hurting.
Your Needs	Take two minutes to pray for God's guidance in your life.

·Day Nineteen·

Psalm 25:12-22
Ethan Jones | Vandalia MetroGroup Leader

This psalm opens by talking about 'those who fear the Lord.' For the longest time, the word fear was confusing for me. How could I love that which I was supposed to fear? But in Scripture, fear quite often refers to a "reverent awe." This psalm is beautiful in that it shows us that our fear of the Lord is what helps us to have the faith to know that God is our source of victory over the troubles of this world, and not ourselves. Proverbs 9:10 says that "the fear of the Lord is the beginning of wisdom" and wisdom is what we see from this psalm of David as he lives out this fear of the Lord.

In these verses, we see the relationship God offers to those who fear him. Verse 13 tells us we will live in prosperity and have a secure future. Verse 14 tells us the Lord is a friend to those who fear him. Verse 15 tells us the Lord will rescue us from the traps of our enemies. As the psalm goes on we see David recognize his need for God to help in David's distress and to forgive his sins. We see David begging for God's protection. Why would he do this? He fears the Lord and has a relationship with God and understands who God truly is.

So how do we apply this psalm to our own lives? Fear of the Lord means God is first in our lives. We give up control over our lives and trust where God will lead us. In verse 15 David speaks of his eyes always being on the Lord. There are so many traps and temptations in the world trying to take us from God, and we have to sustain our desire for God by keeping our focus on HIm. Going back to the words 'fear' and 'wisdom' we see in this psalm that the fear of the Lord helped David with the wisdom to know it was God alone who would rescue David. Let us pray for a "reverent awe" of the Lord from whom our rescue comes.

Facilitated Prayer:

Find a location where you can focus your mind and calm your spirit as you move into a time of prayer. Spend the next few minutes using the P-R-A-Y prompts to enter into a conversation with God. The prompts are to help focus your time of prayer by taking the guesswork out of who and what to pray about each day.

·Day Nineteen·

PRAY:

Praise	Take one minute to be in "reverent awe" of God.
Repent	Take one minute to admit where God has not been first place in your life.
Ask for Others	Take two minutes to pray for those who are in need of the wisdom which comes from having a reverent awe of God.
Your Needs	Take two minutes to give God complete control and surrender to specific circumstances and relationships in your life.

Taking Notes:

_____

_____

_____

_____

_____

_____

_____

_____

_____

_____

_____

Psalm 31:14-24
Corie Book | Edwardsville MetroGroup Leader

Can you relate to David in these verses? Can you relate to the feelings of opposition, attack, panic? Maybe you are thinking back on a time when you felt anguish or despair, or maybe you don't have to think back at all. You might currently be in a place of struggle.

David was obviously facing a lot of opposition and difficulties when he wrote this psalm. In my mind, he had two choices of response. He could blame God for his circumstances and be angry that God was allowing such hardship in his life, OR he could choose to focus on who God is – His character.

David chose the latter. Instead of projecting his circumstances onto the character of God, David chose to remind himself who God is. It can be easy to assume that because our circumstances are bad, God is not good. It can be easy to assume that because we struggle, God isn't listening or doesn't care. But to assume those things would go against the very word of God – God is trustworthy and good. David reminds himself that God's love is unfailing and He hears our cries. And, since we know that God is immutable (unchanging), we can be sure that the same faithful, loving, trustworthy God hears our cries as well.

When the inevitable storms of life come, we can learn from David's example. Pour out your heart to God. Tell Him about all the despair, panic and anxiety you are experiencing. And then, focus on who He is. Praise Him for His character and allow His presence to shelter you.

Facilitated Prayer:

Find a location where you can focus your mind and calm your spirit as you move into a time of prayer. Spend the next few minutes using the P-R-A-Y prompts to enter into a conversation with God. The prompts are to help focus your time of prayer by taking the guesswork out of who and what to pray about each day.

·Day 20·

PRAY:

Praise	Take one minute to praise God for His character.
Repent	Take one minute to admit despair, panic and anxiety you are experiencing.
Ask for Others	Take two minutes to pray for those who are struggling and need to know that God is worthy of their trust.
Your Needs	Take two minutes to pour out your heart before God. Ask Him for help concerning the hardship and opposition you are facing.

Taking Notes:

_____

_____

_____

_____

_____

_____

_____

_____

_____

_____

·Day 21·

Psalm 33:1-9
Shirley Young | Edwardsville MetroGroup Leader

Music-we all love music of some kind, whether it's classical, country, hip hop, oldies, etc. Music often helps us identify the feelings we are having, and then helps us take action as we need to.

Have you thought about God's love of music? What is music to God's ears? How can we please Him with our own music?

Of course, we think of our praise music in our worship services. Talented singers and musicians lead us in praising our God, and we sing along. But those of us who can't carry a tune - is God pleased with our off-tune singing? YES!

The God who created the world by speaking it into being is the God who provides our daily needs. The same God who created the deep, beautiful forests creates the paths in our lives as we move through life learning and growing. That same God wants a relationship with us.

How do we praise Him? Of course, we praise Him when we are singing. We praise Him when we are trusting in Him. We praise Him as we acknowledge how awesome and powerful He is.

We praise Him during our quiet time, reading His Word, praying to Him, thanking Him for all He has blessed us with, pouring out our concerns and problems to Him, talking to Him.

Facilitated Prayer:

Find a location where you can focus your mind and calm your spirit as you move into a time of prayer. Spend the next few minutes using the P-R-A-Y prompts to enter into a conversation with God. The prompts are to help focus your time of prayer by taking the guesswork out of who and what to pray about each day.

·Day 21·

PRAY:

Praise	Take one minute to praise God today.
Repent	Take one minute to confess areas of your life where you are complaining instead of praising.
Ask for Others	Take two minutes to pray for those who you know that are overwhelmed with worry or mistrust.
Your Needs	Take two minutes to turn over areas in your life to God, and then praise Him for it.

Taking Notes:

_____

_____

_____

_____

_____

_____

_____

_____

_____

_____

_____

_____

·Day 22·

Psalm 34:1-10
Chris Persons | MetroGroups Central Pastor

Psalm 34 is written by David in which he shares the key to finding joy is by trusting in the Lord. David had just pretended he was crazy in front of King Abimelech and was driven away from the Philistines when he wrote this Psalm.

v.1-3 Blessing the Lord has a profound impact on my soul. It manufactures an internal joy, and it becomes even more joyful when I get to praise the Lord with my church family. When we gather during weekend services and multiple people engage in corporate worship, I literally can feel the manifest presence of the Spirit of God in our midst. There is a power and irreplaceable joy that comes from "exalting His name together"!

v. 4-7 Does God truly deliver me from all "my fears", or my anxious thoughts? There is certainly no shortage of things to fret or be worried about in my life. But as a follower of Christ, I don't have to let my thoughts be held captive by my fears. God promises that if I simply seek and look to Him, He will deliver me. "Pray more, worry less" is the godly prescription my mind and heart truly need.

v. 8-10 The salesman's pitch here is this, "If I sample God, even a little bit, I will not be disappointed. If I try trusting Him, He will not let me down. If I choose to fixate on His goodness, instead of life problems, He will transform my perspective. I will see and experience life differently." At times when I might see a "lack" in my life, God will fill that lack with a "good thing". He may fill it in a different way than I thought or expected, but nonetheless He is faithful. This is a promise I can certainly cling to!

Closing reflection: If I seek Him out through prayer and His Word, then I have nothing to fear. He is faithful, therefore I will not be consumed by worry; but I will be a person who can't help but talk to others about God's goodness in my life and "bless the Lord at all times".

Facilitated Prayer:

Find a location where you can focus your mind and calm your spirit as you move into a time of prayer. Spend the next few minutes using the P-R-A-Y prompts to enter into a conversation with God. The prompts are to help focus your time of prayer by taking the guesswork out of who and what to pray about each day.

·Day 22·

As you "P-R-A-Y..."

PRAY:

Praise	Take one minute to praise God for how He has filled a "lack" in your life in an unexpected way.
Repent	Take one minute to release to God any areas of your life where you have been consumed by worry or anxiety.
Ask for Others	Take two minutes to pray for those who you can talk to about God's goodness in your life.
Your Needs	Take two minutes to ask God to replace your anxious thoughts with trust in Him. Seek Him to deliver you from all your fears.

Taking Notes:

_____

_____

_____

_____

_____

_____

_____

_____

_____

_____

_____

·Day 23·

Psalm 34:11-22
Crystal Persons | Edwardsville MetroGroup Leader

v. 11-14 Fear of the Lord means we fear nothing else. To experience the good, we must proactively turn away from evil. When we "seek peace and pursue it," we make the choice to turn from evil.

v. 15-18 If there was ever a passage of Scripture that communicates Jesus' tender heart for the broken...this is it. The fact that His eyes & ears are toward the righteous means He is FOR us. Verse 18 has guided me through many stormy waters...if Jesus is near to the broken, then it is not a sin to be broken. Being broken does not disqualify me from witnessing & advocating for the good in life... in fact, my brokenness in His hands would cause me to fight all the more for what is good and holy. When my heart is broken for the things that break His heart, I am moved to action. I cannot sit idly by while others suffer.

v. 19-22 My brokenness does not define me...but through it, Jesus proclaims His redemptive power to my heart over and over again. Though I can indeed experience healing in Jesus and must commit myself to that journey with Him, the very brokenness within me will serve as a constant reminder that this world truly does not satisfy. So I desperately turn to Him. It's an ever-present reminder that circumstances can change in the blink of an eye. So I learn to trust His ways above my own. And rather than surrender to fear and condemnation, I lean into my brokenness. I gladly boast of my weaknesses (2 Corinthians 12:9-10) so that His power would be made known THROUGH it. There's no neutral territory, either our brokenness is going to work for us or against us.

Knowing He is near changes absolutely everything. Let's stop despising our brokenness and hiding it away. Know His peace and pursue it by spending time together with Him regularly.

PRAY your way through a passage of Scripture.

PRAY when you feel fearful.

PRAY that He would open your eyes to the ways you have stopped fighting for what's good in life because you've been broken.

He wants to redeem or "buy back" your brokenness to be used FOR YOU and not against you. Peace always comes in the surrender, and freedom through His redemption. What good could come from us being truly free?? Well, that's a God-sized answer.

·Day 23·

Facilitated Prayer:

Find a location where you can focus your mind and calm your spirit as you move into a time of prayer. Spend the next few minutes using the P-R-A-Y prompts to enter into a conversation with God. The prompts are to help focus your time of prayer by taking the guesswork out of who and what to pray about each day.

As you "P-R-A-Y..."

PRAY:

Praise	Take one minute to praise God in your brokenness.
Repent	Take one minute to release from being defined by your brokenness.
Ask for Others	Take two minutes to pray for those who are struggling with brokenness that you can lift up to God today.
Your Needs	Take two minutes to ask God to help you rest in His peace.

Taking Notes:

_____

_____

_____

_____

_____

Psalm 37:3-7
Colleen Fender | Vandalia MetroGroup Leader

Sometimes relationships fail. Sometimes you can't depend on other people, and that hurts. Has this ever happened to you? Thinking back over the span of your life, how many times can you identify where someone disappointed you; or, how many times do you think you have disappointed someone else?

The reality is, being human, we are going to make mistakes. We are going to do things wrong sometimes, and unfortunately, we are going to hurt peoples' feelings sometimes as well.

Learning how to trust in the Lord is a key to healing these hurts. Building your relationship with Jesus happens in many ways – through prayer, through reading the Bible, through community with other believers – and each of those things help you develop your confidence in Him.

Psalm 36:3-7 tells us several ways to accomplish this: to trust in the Lord, take delight in the Lord, commit your way to the Lord, and to be still before the Lord.

Committing more time to prayer and having a growing prayer life not only shows our trust in Jesus, but also shows how we take delight in Him. Over time, those times of prayer with God turn into a trusted friendship with Him and will allow you to be comfortable in the stillness of prayer.

Strengthening our ability to pray continuously will make us a better friend to others – one who is more apt to think before they speak, and less likely to hurt and disappoint our friends and family.

Facilitated Prayer:

Find a location where you can focus your mind and calm your spirit as you move into a time of prayer. Spend the next few minutes using the P-R-A-Y prompts to enter into a conversation with God. The prompts are to help focus your time of prayer by taking the guesswork out of who and what to pray about each day.

·Day 24·

PRAY:

Praise	Take one minute to praise God for how He delights in providing for you.
Repent	Take one minute to invite God into healing your past hurts.
Ask for Others	Take two minutes to pray for those who need to discover God's eagerness to bless their life.
Your Needs	Take two minutes to ask God to help you to be still and be a person of continuous prayer.

Taking Notes:

Psalm 37:23-24
Fred Francis | Edwardsville MetroGroup Leader

How does a child of God "pray" the 37th Psalm?
Make sure that you are a child of God through a relationship with Jesus. Rom 10:9

Purify your faith – Psalms 37:28 states, "For the Lord loves justice and will not abandon His faithful ones. They are kept safe forever, but the children of the wicked will be destroyed." Hebrews 11:6 goes on to say, "But without faith ("the substance of things hoped for but not seen") it is impossible to please God." David goes on to say, "The wicked one lies in wait for the righteous and intends to kill him; the Lord will not leave him in the power of the wicked one or allow him to be condemned when he is judged." Faith, however, may need to be tested in the fires of adversity. Faith is essential for praying and living the Christian life because the ways of God are opposite to the natural inclinations of man.

Confess your sin – Psalms 37:28 warns, "but the children of the wicked will be destroyed." "If I regard iniquity in my heart, the Lord will not hear me." Psalms 66:18

Forsake your sin – Psalms 37:23 tells us, "a person's steps are established by the Lord and He takes pleasure in His ways," and Paul adds, "Let us walk with decency, not carousing and drunkenness, not in sexual impurity, not in quarreling and jealousy. But put on the Lord Jesus, and make no provision for the flesh to gratify its desires." Romans 13:13-14

Know your God – Psalms 37:34 encourages us to "Wait on the Lord and keep His ways and He will exalt you," and Paul adds, "...all power and authority come from God." Romans 13:1

Get your facts – Understand what you are asking of God. Pray specifically, not in general. Proverbs 18:13

Resist the enemy – Psalms 37:32 warns, "The wicked lie in wait for the righteous and intends to kill him;" Ask God to keep Satan from tempting you and confusing your mind.

Express your thanks to God – "Be careful for nothing; but in every thing by prayer and supplication with thanksgiving let your request be made known to God." Philippians 4:6

·Day 25·

Facilitated Prayer:

Find a location where you can focus your mind and calm your spirit as you move into a time of prayer. Spend the next few minutes using the P-R-A-Y prompts to enter into a conversation with God. The prompts are to help focus your time of prayer by taking the guesswork out of who and what to pray about each day.

As you "P-R-A-Y..."

PRAY:

Praise	Take one minute to thank God for His amazing grace which provides us with the faith we need.
Repent	Take one minute to confess if you have lacked spending intentional time in prayer.
Ask for Others	Take two minutes to pray for those who need help to become more strategic in the way they read Scripture and pray.
Your Needs	Take two minutes to meditate and ask God's help with becoming more adept at reading His Word and praying with faith.

Taking Notes:

_____

_____

_____

_____

_____

Psalm 40:1-5
Bridget Christner | Edwardsville MetroGroup Leader

"I've got this." If you're anything like me, you've uttered this phrase a time or two. When facing any challenge or adversity, it's easy to default to wanting to take care of things ourselves – to rely on our strengths and capabilities. We think this will grant us an immediate resolution, but "immediate" is not always better.

When we take our troubles to God first, we don't always get an instant response nor do we always get the response that we want. But we do get the answer we need, and we get it at the exact moment we need it. Because when God moves, He moves. And God doesn't just change our circumstances. He changes our hearts. When we show up, when we wait on the Lord, when we trust His plan and His power and His goodness – He not only sees us and hears us and brings us out of the "desolate pit," but He also transforms us.

Continually going to God in prayer and thanksgiving reminds us of what He has done in our lives and what He can do. The more we seek God out, the more we see Him daily. And when we see Him, we praise Him. And suddenly, when life gets hard, when things don't pan out the way we'd like them to, our hearts have changed because we know that whatever we face, God is bigger and greater than it all.

"How happy is anyone who has put his trust in the Lord and has not turned to the proud or to those who run after lies!"

So, whatever is going on in your life, instead of saying, "I've got this," know that you have an awesome, powerful, and mighty God that never changes, never falters, and has such wondrous plans for you. He will never fail, and He is always good. God's got this!

Facilitated Prayer:

Find a location where you can focus your mind and calm your spirit as you move into a time of prayer. Spend the next few minutes using the P-R-A-Y prompts to enter into a conversation with God. The prompts are to help focus your time of prayer by taking the guesswork out of who and what to pray about each day.

·Day 26·

As you "P-R-A-Y..."

PRAY:

Praise	Take one minute to praise God for a "pit" He has recently lifted you from.
Repent	Take one minute to surrender any areas where you are saying "I've got this".
Ask for Others	Take two minutes to pray for those who you know who need to be drawn out of a "desolate pit".
Your Needs	Take two minutes to wait patiently for the Lord through prayer instead of seeking an immediate solution by yourself.

Taking Notes:

_____

_____

_____

_____

_____

_____

_____

_____

_____

_____

_____

·Day 27·

Psalm 42:1-11
Bethany Bell | Edwardsville MetroGroup Leader

Desperation is not really an enjoyable emotion. That overwhelming feeling that your circumstances are beyond you, beyond what you can do within your own strength. If we're honest, most of us go to great lengths to avoid looking or feeling desperate, but life on this side of heaven often leads us to places of desperation no matter how much we do to guard against them. I have been there – when the ultrasound showed something was going to be wrong with my baby or when family drama led to division and painful words that still hurt.

It's those moments that remind us that hope in ourselves is fruitless because control over our circumstances is limited. In those moments, what do we do? The psalmist suggests in Psalm 42 that we remember. We remember His steadfast love. We remember He is our rock. We remember His song is with us in the actual and metaphorical night, even when we don't feel it. We remember past moments of joy overflowing into praise and worship of our God. We place our hope in His track record of showing up and His unlimited, unmatched, inexhaustible power.

Is there any better place to be than desperate for God to show up, desperate for Him to move, desperate for His presence? If we really believe that He is Lord and we are not, then we have to ask ourselves: are we really better off when we feel like "We got this"? Circumstances that lead us to desperation and the moments we spend in desperation can be a kind of grace. When we allow these moments to bring us to our knees in prayer, they draw us into surrender and into Him. They bring us to the only place of power we truly have, petitioning our loving God to be with us and to act and respond on our behalf. In prayer we remember, we hope, and we wait on the God who has proven himself present, loving, and worthy of praise.

Let's pray to remember as the psalmist suggests. Use the time in prayer to praise the many names and characteristics of God that have been present in the lives of others or yourself.

Facilitated Prayer:

Find a location where you can focus your mind and calm your spirit as you move into a time of prayer. Spend the next few minutes using the P-R-A-Y prompts to enter into a conversation with God. The prompts are to help focus your time of prayer by taking the guesswork out of who and what to pray about each day.

·Day 27·

PRAY:

Praise	Take one minute to start listing God's attributes (A to Z)? Plan another time to finish your list.
Repent	Take one minute to assess if in moments of hurt and desperation you turn outward, inward, or upward.
Ask for Others	Take two minutes to pray for those who need to know that you are joining them on your knees, remembering them.
Your Needs	Take two minutes to dwell on the attributes of God that will help you through a current time of desperation in your life.

Taking Notes:

_____

_____

_____

_____

_____

_____

_____

_____

_____

_____

_____

·Day 28·

Psalm 46:1-11
Micheal & Stacey Pace | Edwardsville MetroGroup Leaders

We've all been there at some point in our life. Looking back, maybe it was something minor. Maybe not...maybe it was a huge, life changing event. Either way, at that moment, you felt as though your world was shaken and possibly collapsing. The key with any event in life isn't about what the circumstances were, but how we responded.

So, when the mountains quake and the waters roar, what's your response? Do you throw your hands up in the air and run in circles screaming? Do you retreat into a room of the house and ask everyone to leave you alone? Maybe you try to numb the pain or concern by having a few too many drinks alone or with friends. Do you become harsh to those around you? There is something that all these things have in common. They do absolutely nothing to solve the problem.

As a follower of Christ, acknowledge that it is by His grace that we are saved. We profess our belief that He is all powerful and all knowing. We tell others that God will help them in their time of need and that we will be praying for them, but do we follow our own advice when it is our world that is shaken? Turn to God, fully trusting that He already knows how our situation ends and works all things for the good of those who love Him (Romans 8:28).

Our hope...our help...our peace...our better future...they come from the Lord. Don't allow yourself to give in to earthly doubts about the power of God. He is our strength and never leaves us. He is Yahweh Sabaoth, the Lord of Hosts, the commander of the heavenly armies. He is for us, and nothing can stand in the way of that. Run to him daily as your refuge and strength. Pour out your praise to Him. Voice your prayers and concerns to Him. And, as it states in verse 10, "Be still, and know that I am God....".

Facilitated Prayer:

Find a location where you can focus your mind and calm your spirit as you move into a time of prayer. Spend the next few minutes using the P-R-A-Y prompts to enter into a conversation with God. The prompts are to help focus your time of prayer by taking the guesswork out of who and what to pray about each day.

·Day 28·

PRAY:

Praise	Take one minute to thank God for being your refuge and strength.
Repent	Take one minute to hand God your fears in exchange for His rest.
Ask for Others	Take two minutes to pray for those who you know that need to know that God is for them.
Your Needs	Take two minutes to "be still" and acknowledge God's power over all situations in your life.

Taking Notes:

_____

_____

_____

_____

_____

_____

_____

_____

_____

_____

_____

Psalm 51:1-12

Cassidy Awalt | Vandalia MetroGroup Leader

Yuck! It happened again – that same sin that has been a thorn in your side, that same temptation you always give in to, those thoughts and temptations that just won't go away and you couldn't say no any longer. So, there you sit in your guilt and shame. This is a familiar place. This is a place where you've either begged God for forgiveness and help or you've turned away from the Lord trying to hide because you are too ashamed. You've walked with the Lord, and you know His way. You say to yourself, "This shouldn't keep happening."

King David is experiencing those same feelings of guilt and shame when he pleads before the Lord in Psalm 51:1-12. King David, who was described as a "man after God's own heart," is trapped in sin's consequence. He committed adultery with Bathsheba. King David at first tries to cover up his sin until the shame and conviction become too much to bear. In this psalm, King David confesses his sin and pleads before the Lord to blot out his transgressions, to wash him clean, to purify his heart.

How many times have you tried to hide in your sin because the guilt and shame were too much to bear? How many times have you tried to keep your temptations and sins hidden from everyone else because you're supposed to be a "good Christian," and what would people think if they found out? Or worse yet, would God still choose to love and use you?

When you come before the Lord and repent of your sin, He welcomes you with open arms. The Good Father wants to wash you white as snow as He sets you free from that thorn in your side. So pray today the words of King David, "Create in me a clean heart, O God. Renew a loyal spirit within me. Do not banish me from your presence, and don't take your Holy Spirit from me. Restore me to the joy of your salvation and make me willing to obey you." Psalm 51:10-12

Facilitated Prayer:

Find a location where you can focus your mind and calm your spirit as you move into a time of prayer. Spend the next few minutes using the P-R-A-Y prompts to enter into a conversation with God. The prompts are to help focus your time of prayer by taking the guesswork out of who and what to pray about each day.

·Day 29·

As you "P-R-A-Y..."

PRAY:

Praise	Take one minute to thank God for His desire to forgive you and allow you to approach Him in prayer.
Repent	Take one minute to confess any sins that continue to be a thorn in your side.
Ask for Others	Take two minutes to pray for someone who needs to know that God is a forgiving God.
Your Needs	Take two minutes to ask God to create within you a clean heart and to restore the joy of your salvation through obedience.

Taking Notes:

_____

_____

_____

_____

_____

_____

_____

_____

_____

_____

_____

·Day 30·

Psalm 56:1-11
Matt Bearly | Edwardsville MetroGroup Leader

Why is this happening to me? Why would they treat me this way? Why do I feel so far from the life I envisioned? Why me, God?

The grass is greener on the other side...right? It is easy to get caught up in that mindset and begin to believe the lies that the world tells us. You need this house, car, gadget, etc. You should make this much money. You should have accomplished _____ by now! Other people don't have the problems that you have. Everyone else has already done x, y, and z; when will you? Maybe you aren't worthy. Maybe you aren't cut out for it. Maybe you should just give up.

MAYBE NOT. Maybe the grass isn't greener on the other side, maybe it is greener where you water it. Are you watering the fields of negative thoughts and emotions in your life, or, are you watering the endless expanse of promises that God has made to love you, protect you, and care for you?

Romans 12:2 reminds us, 'Do not conform to the pattern of this world, but be transformed by the renewing of your mind. Then you will be able to test and approve what God's will is—his good, pleasing and perfect will.' God has promised to never leave you, to rescue and protect you and give you strength, to free you from sin, to hear your prayers and make all things come together for your good, and to love you for eternity. But, you must believe it to be able to tap into the power that comes from Him.

So today, make a choice to not allow the lies to distract you from what God wants to do in and through your life. Instead of asking "Why me?" when adversity hits, think "Why not me?!". Why not let God use me to be a beacon of hope, a light in the dark, and a force for his kingdom? Choose to trust God with your life and let your actions flow from that heartbeat to water the fields of positivity and abundance that He has promised! Life happens for you, not to you, and everything is either God sent or God used.

Facilitated Prayer:

Find a location where you can focus your mind and calm your spirit as you move into a time of prayer. Spend the next few minutes using the P-R-A-Y prompts to enter into a conversation with God. The prompts are to help focus your time of prayer by taking the guesswork out of who and what to pray about each day.

·Day 30·

PRAY:

Praise	Take one minute to praise God for the difficult circumstances you are experiencing.
Repent	Take one minute to repent for a time you took your eyes off Him and doubted your faith.
Ask for Others	Take two minutes to pray for someone you know who is battling fear.
Your Needs	Take two minutes to talk to God about the "enemies" in your life and then put your trust in Him to protect you.

Taking Notes:

_____

_____

_____

_____

_____

_____

_____

_____

_____

_____

_____

Psalm 57:4-11
Anonymous | Edwardsville MetroGroup Leader

When reading Psalm 57:4, all feels hopeless. Being surrounded by lions or people whose words are like sharp swords would be absolutely awful. And yet how often we may feel that many situations in our lives are like a devouring lion or a big trap that we are about to fall into.

A young lady recently shared her story with me. It started with an awful situation that was out of her control. It affected her in traumatic ways and sadly she fell into a pit of depression and drugs, among other horrific events that happened to her over the course of a couple of years. She had grown up in a Christian home yet felt so far from God and His love and questioned how He could love her now.

While the psalm starts off hopeless like this lady's situation, as we continue reading, the situation and mood shifts. "They dug a pit ahead of me but they themselves fell into it." (Psalm 57: 6b) God is always working and fighting on our behalf in hopes that we will turn to Him in the midst of life's struggles and temptations.

This young lady's story also shifted when another woman with a similar past poured into her and shared that her story doesn't have to stop there. God is bigger. She clung onto that and several verses in the Bible. She has since rededicated her life to Christ and sees the power in her own life of His love that is as high as the heavens and His faithfulness that reaches to the sky.

The writer of this psalm, while battling distress, saw God's hand in the situation and chose to be confident in who God says He is through worshiping and singing praises to the Lord. We can do the same. By the end of this psalm, we are reminded that no matter the situation or outcome, God's love and faithfulness are greater than we can imagine and we can trust that He is worthy of our prayers and praise.

Facilitated Prayer:

Find a location where you can focus your mind and calm your spirit as you move into a time of prayer. Spend the next few minutes using the P-R-A-Y prompts to enter into a conversation with God. The prompts are to help focus your time of prayer by taking the guesswork out of who and what to pray about each day.

·Day 31·

PRAY:

Praise	Take one minute to rejoice in how you see God's steadfast love in your life.
Repent	Take one minute to repent of times you felt hopeless in your life and took matters into your own hands.
Ask for Others	Take two minutes to pray for those you know who are "in the midst of lions".
Your Needs	Take two minutes to pray about situations in your life that feel like you yourself are "in the midst of lions."

Taking Notes:

_____

_____

_____

_____

_____

_____

_____

_____

_____

_____

_____

·Day 32·

Psalm 61:1-8
Scott Giles | Edwardsville MetroGroup Leader

I was blessed to be raised by parents who were strong Christians and did their best to show Christ-like love to others. They provided me with fantastic examples of how followers of Christ are called to live, and their love of God was evident to those who encountered them during their time on this earth. They taught me early on, however, that as deep as their love for God was, it could not approach the depth of His love for them.

As I read Psalm 61, I find references to the following biblical truths relating to God's love and character I have witnessed in their lives and mine.

God is available. God hears our prayers no matter where we are in life. Be it a time in which we are overwhelmed or a time that we are searching for guidance or direction.

God is our refuge. There is safety and unimaginable peace on hand for the children of God. We are called not to worry, but rather to bring our petitions to Him in prayer and to do so with a thankful heart.

God's inheritance awaits us. Those who confess their sins and accept Jesus Christ as their Savior, receive eternal life. Best of all, our eternal life will be spent with our Father in Heaven.

Let's be mindful not to just enjoy the blessings these truths bring us. We should praise God's name and thank him for His love during our prayer time and then fulfill our vows of obedience to Him and love for others as we live day-to-day.

Facilitated Prayer:

Find a location where you can focus your mind and calm your spirit as you move into a time of prayer. Spend the next few minutes using the P-R-A-Y prompts to enter into a conversation with God. The prompts are to help focus your time of prayer by taking the guesswork out of who and what to pray about each day.

·Day 32·

PRAY:

Praise	Take one minute to praise God for His love for us.
Repent	Take one minute to confess any broken or forgotten vows that are hindering your walk with God.
Ask for Others	Take two minutes to pray for those who need to be reminded that God is only a prayer away.
Your Needs	Take two minutes to discuss with God how you will remain consistent in performing your vows of obedience day after day.

Taking Notes:

_____

_____

_____

_____

_____

_____

_____

_____

_____

_____

_____

·Day 33·

Psalm 62:1-8
Scott & Marianna Weber | Edwardsville MetroGroup Leaders

How often do we see job interests, the want for power, the chase of money, as an attempt to find happiness? We see this lack of fulfillment daily in the news, in the paper, and in relationships within the community.

Be still and trust in God. As the day begins it is often difficult to be still. Family concerns, work issues, and community problems can quickly consume and burden our hearts and thoughts. Then the cell phone rings, or text/emails arrive which can create immediate concern. Worrying and daily tasks can easily overcome our mind. Our first focus needs to be trust in God. As David stated in verse 1 of Psalm 62, "My soul finds rest in God alone".

It is hard to wait on God. If you have ever had an active pet, in our case an Australian Shepherd Border Collie mix, it is difficult to teach pets to wait. Just like our dog, Nacho, our human nature makes it very difficult to wait. Here, David is most likely in exile, trying to avoid King Saul's army. Yet David finds peace in putting his whole trust in God. It is by the grace of God that He waits and never gives up. David found peace by putting his whole trust in God. David also authored Psalm 29:11: "The Lord gives strength to his people; The Lord blesses his people with peace."

Don't hold anything back, "Pour out your hearts before him." David shares his peace with others and encourages them through this psalm. As a leader of God's people, he reinforced basic truths. A very important one being that God is worthy at all times of our trust, which includes times of sorrow and joy. We are blessed by God's word, our church community, and prayer which strengthen our faith and trust in God.

Facilitated Prayer:

Find a location where you can focus your mind and calm your spirit as you move into a time of prayer. Spend the next few minutes using the P-R-A-Y prompts to enter into a conversation with God. The prompts are to help focus your time of prayer by taking the guesswork out of who and what to pray about each day.

·Day 33·

As you "P-R-A-Y..."

PRAY:

Praise	Take one minute to express your gratitude for the eternal trustworthiness of God.
Repent	Take one minute to confess a recent time you got impatient with God and chose to trust in yourself instead of Him.
Ask for Others	Take two minutes to pray for those who need to place their trust in God through some very difficult circumstances.
Your Needs	Take two minutes to replace worrisome thoughts with trust and faith in God's plans.

Taking Notes:

_____

_____

_____

_____

_____

_____

_____

_____

_____

_____

_____

_____

Psalm 63:1-8

Anonymous | Edwardsville MetroGroup Leader

When David wrote this psalm, he was in the wilderness of Judah desperately on the run from King Saul who, along with 2,000 of his soldiers, relentlessly pursued David in order to kill him. David was innocent of any crime against King Saul or against Israel, but Saul was driven by his out-of-control jealousy of David. Though David had a band of 600 men with him (I Samuel 23:13), he did not rely on them for security; instead, he sought the One he knew intimately.

We see the "man after God's own heart" seeking in fervent prayer his God whom he desires more than life. God is his delight, his sanctuary, and his provider in this stressful situation. His prayerful seeking turns to joyful praise as he declares his soul is satisfied with abundance when he meditates on his faithful God and recognizes God is his help. David's circumstances hadn't changed but his heart was filled with joy.

As Believers, we have the same relationship with God as David celebrated. When difficulties arise, we can pour out our heart to Him in our need. As we do, He turns our fear and anxiety to praise and worship – a beautiful exchange. While we are told in God's Word, "Let your requests be made known to God," prayer is really about who God is. Praise and worship of God drive away the negative thoughts that block our focus on our Jehovah Jireh. It is always appropriate to praise the Lord. It doesn't matter where we are; it doesn't matter how we feel.

In this passage David writes, "Your right hand upholds me;" and in Psalm 73:23 we read, "You hold me by my right hand." The scene is of God's own right hand holding our right hand – picture that, we are held fast and face to face with our God and Savior!! Selah…

Facilitated Prayer:

Find a location where you can focus your mind and calm your spirit as you move into a time of prayer. Spend the next few minutes using the P-R-A-Y prompts to enter into a conversation with God. The prompts are to help focus your time of prayer by taking the guesswork out of who and what to pray about each day.

·Day 34·

PRAY:

Praise	Take one minute to celebrate a time when you felt outnumbered, but God sustained you with His "right hand".
Repent	Take one minute to repent of times you see yourself as a victim of circumstances instead of an ally of God.
Ask for Others	Take two minutes to pray for those who need to learn the art of trading anxiety for adoration.
Your Needs	Take two minutes to ask for God's help with interpreting your circumstances this week as opportunities instead of obstacles.

Taking Notes:

_____

_____

_____

_____

_____

_____

_____

_____

_____

_____

_____

·Day 35·

Psalm 66:1-5
Ryan Heard | Edwardsville MetroGroup Leader

We all love a great victory after a hard-fought battle. I enjoy seeing sports videos of buzzer beater shots, walk off home runs, winning touchdowns, and photo-finish races. In US history, we have the sorrow-filled joy of having won a Revolutionary War to establish our independence from Great Britain, a Civil War to end slavery, and World Wars to end German and Japanese occupation of other nations. However, our battles are usually personal ones such as being cured of a disease, regained mobility after an injury, overcoming an addiction, receiving a favorable court ruling, obedience from your unruly child, getting out of credit card debt, employment after a job loss, and many more. These personal victories are amazing and bring about feelings of ecstatic joy.

Psalm 66 reaffirms that God answers prayer both individually and as a body of Believers. Verses 1-5 set the tone that we should have an energetic expression of worship and gratitude for the marvelous victories through our mighty God. Our worship should not be restrained or half-hearted, but filled with joy and enthusiasm. As we contemplate the greatness of God and the wonders He has accomplished, our hearts should overflow with gratitude, compelling us to give Him the magnificent praise He deserves. The Lord's awe-inspiring power will even bring those who oppose Him to their knees. This is a strong reminder that God is not to be taken lightly or underestimated and that His power reigns supreme over all creation.

Today, let us respond to the psalmist's call to glorify God and sing praises to His name. Let our worship be characterized by joy, awe, and gratitude. May we take time to reflect on the Lord's amazing works and invite others to join us in celebrating His greatness. As we do, we will experience a deeper sense of connection with our heavenly Father and encounter the transformative power of His presence in our lives.

Facilitated Prayer:

Find a location where you can focus your mind and calm your spirit as you move into a time of prayer. Spend the next few minutes using the P-R-A-Y prompts to enter into a conversation with God. The prompts are to help focus your time of prayer by taking the guesswork out of who and what to pray about each day.

·Day 35·

PRAY:

Praise	Take one minute to worship God through joy, awe, and gratitude.
Repent	Take one minute to admit to God if your prayer life has been lackluster.
Ask for Others	Take two minutes to pray for those who need to hear how God is impacting your daily life through answered prayers.
Your Needs	Take two minutes to ask God to help you develop a deeper sense of connection with Him this week.

Taking Notes:

·Day 36·

Psalm 71:1-6
Lauren Sczurko | Edwardsville MetroGroup Leader

Refuge is defined as a safe place. The word refuge is used twice in the first three verses of Psalm 71. In the Bible, when a word is repeated it is important. The unknown author of this Psalm is reflecting on his life and how God was always with him. What a beautiful display of faith the author shows when at the end of his life he is continuing to seek refuge in God.

Our lives are a testimony of what God has done for us. When the author of Psalm 71 is reflecting on his testimony he sees that God is a safe place, a just God and our living hope. God will use our stories to help others know Him.

Is God your refuge?
How does your testimony bring Him glory? If you have never done so, write your testimony down. Then you will be prepared to share about our good God.

God is a safe place to which you can turn. He will never leave you (Hebrews 13:5). Rest in His promises today.

Facilitated Prayer:

Find a location where you can focus your mind and calm your spirit as you move into a time of prayer. Spend the next few minutes using the P-R-A-Y prompts to enter into a conversation with God. The prompts are to help focus your time of prayer by taking the guesswork out of who and what to pray about each day.

·Day 36·

As you "P-R-A-Y..."

PRAY:

Praise	Take one minute to praise God for how He has shown Himself faithful to you this past week.
Repent	Take one minute to confess ways you are not allowing God to be your refuge.
Ask for Others	Take two minutes to ask God to reveal who you need to share your God story with, so they can also come to know Him as a place of refuge.
Your Needs	Take two minutes to pray about how you can lean into God as your refuge today.

Taking Notes:

_____

_____

_____

_____

_____

_____

_____

_____

_____

_____

_____

Psalm 73:18-26
Caeden Barron | Metro Ministry Resident

Do you ever feel like the enemy is winning? Like the world is out to get you and weighing down on you with every step? As the days go on ,you feel yourself slowly but surely slipping to a sea of depression, a mass of lies on your shoulders, or just the desire to lay in your bed and never wake up.

Do not be dismayed. God has made our enemies live in a world worse than ours, a world where they are the ones who should fear death, destruction, and terror. Though they may come at us with fighting words and evil motives, God will surely destroy them when the time is right.

We have assurance that God overcomes opposition, but you also do not have to live with the perspective that God is disappointed in you in the midst of battles. Repent and show him that you know the enemy never was more powerful than Him. Tell Him though you did not acknowledge He was there, He was always present. God has shielded you from a worse reality than the one you feared at the time, eternal suffering, and saved you from a life permanently separated from Him. Tell Him you need His security, His intentionality, His love. Know that He will receive you again and again, with open arms and tears of joy in His eyes. Remember that God is more powerful than anything that comes against you, whether height or depth, or evil powers, or time itself; He is stronger. Come to Him and find peace in His infinite serenity, and remember, it is good to be near God.

Facilitated Prayer:

Find a location where you can focus your mind and calm your spirit as you move into a time of prayer. Spend the next few minutes using the P-R-A-Y prompts to enter into a conversation with God. The prompts are to help focus your time of prayer by taking the guesswork out of who and what to pray about each day.

·Day 37·

PRAY:

Praise	Take one minute to celebrate God's guarantee of ultimate victory in life's battles.
Repent	Take one minute to repent of times when you were envious of the wicked.
Ask for Others	Take two minutes to pray for those who are in a battle...that they would not be dismayed but find God's infinite serenity.
Your Needs	Take two minutes to draw near to God and ask Him for His security, His intentionality, and His love in your life.

Taking Notes:

_____

_____

_____

_____

_____

_____

_____

_____

_____

_____

_____

·Day 38·

Psalm 74:18-23
Erica Donoho | Edwardsville MetroGroup Leader

Rise up, O God! Do You see the evil in this world? How can You ignore it? It is everywhere I look! Sometimes it feels that God isn't paying attention to the events happening in this world.

We feel pain in this life. We watch our family and friends suffer, and we wonder how God does not act. Let's be honest, we want judgment. We want to see the evil things destroyed and revel in the triumph of victory! We have a deep longing for the heartache of this world to be overcome.

The wonderful thing is that it HAS been overcome! God sent Jesus to die for us, and through His resurrection He secured the defeat of death and evil (John 16:33). As we cry out to God, He invites us to remember who He is and what He has done.

Deuteronomy 4:31, "For the LORD your God is a merciful God; he will not abandon you or destroy you or forget the covenant with your forefathers, which he confirmed to you by oath."

His covenant is to never leave us and to prosper us. He will not leave us in our distress. He will not leave the world in a state of chaos with evil, darkness, and violence. He remembers His covenant with His people. God is paying attention; He cares for His people, and His plans are greater than anything we can imagine.

Revelation 21:4-5a, "He will wipe every tear from their eyes. There will be no more death or mourning or crying or pain, for the old order of things has passed away. He who was seated on the throne said, 'I am making all things new!' "

Cry out to God! Tell Him about the things overwhelming your family, tell Him your fears about the evil in our world, trust in His power, and rest assured of His victory over evil.

Facilitated Prayer:

Find a location where you can focus your mind and calm your spirit as you move into a time of prayer. Spend the next few minutes using the P-R-A-Y prompts to enter into a conversation with God. The prompts are to help focus your time of prayer by taking the guesswork out of who and what to pray about each day.

·Day 38·

PRAY:

Praise	Take one minute to thank God for our eternal victory over sin!
Repent	Take one minute to surrender times you have fallen as a victim to this world instead of being an overcomer through Christ.
Ask for Others	Take two minutes to pray for those who are overwhelmed by life and need to experience God's power and victory.
Your Needs	Take two minutes to tell God your fears about the evil in this world and submit your trust in Him.

Taking Notes:

_____

_____

_____

_____

_____

_____

_____

_____

_____

_____

_____

·Day 39·

Psalm 77:1-10
Brian Dossett | Vandalia MetroGroup Leader

If you are like me you will cry out to God for help when you feel desperately powerless! You need a dramatic divine intervention and you need it now! Perhaps a loved one is in sudden danger or experienced a horrible tragedy. Maybe you just found out that you have some life altering health problem like cancer or major heart disease. Or it could be that you just discovered that your child is in a life or death struggle with alcohol or another addiction. Situations like these are thrust upon us and we get scared or angry. We cannot control the outcome so we cry out to God for help, just like the psalmist in Psalm 77.

I can relate to crying out to God when I desperately need His help, and I can also relate to seeking the Lord at night. I have spent many long hours into the night pleading with the Lord for wisdom, guidance, comfort, or for absolute spiritual intervention. I have felt compelled by God to pray on behalf of a person or situation, and I have felt that God kept my eyes from closing. Sometimes my final prayer is that God would mercifully release me from my troubled spirit so that I could get some sleep!

Some trials I go through are prolonged and intense, and if I don't get the response to my prayers that I am hoping for, I may wonder if God is really listening or even cares. But honestly, if doubts do arise, I have learned to remind myself how often God has intervened in my life through prayer. God gave us three precious children through adoption when we could have no children of our own. He has healed many people in my practice that cannot be explained by medical science. The most dramatic answered prayer witnessed by my own physician eyes was what God did for my wife, Laura, who collapsed on the high school track and was dead for seventeen minutes. Through the intense prayer of many people, I saw the miracle of Laura coming back to life, without any brain damage, which is absolutely inexplicable. I spent two long restless nights crying out to God in anguish for my wife, and God was gracious beyond belief. God will not answer every prayer the way we hope, but He will be with us always as we cry out to him for help.

Facilitated Prayer:

Find a location where you can focus your mind and calm your spirit as you move into a time of prayer. Spend the next few minutes using the P-R-A-Y prompts to enter into a conversation with God. The prompts are to help focus your time of prayer by taking the guesswork out of who and what to pray about each day.

·Day 39·

PRAY:

Praise	Take one minute to praise God for hearing your cries!
Repent	Take one minute to cry out to God about whatever troubles your spirit so you can find rest in Him.
Ask for Others	Take two minutes to pray for those who need to be reminded of God's past faithfulness during a present crisis.
Your Needs	Take two minutes to reflect on God's past faithfulness so you can experience His strength for your current struggles.

Taking Notes:

_____

_____

_____

_____

_____

_____

_____

_____

_____

_____

_____

_____

·Day 40·

Psalm 77:10-20
Laura Dossett | Vandalia MetroGroup Leader

In the first half of this psalm, the writer is distressed, desperate for God to help him; he is so upset that he can't sleep or even talk about it. He repeatedly begs God to help him, but he receives no answer. He wonders if God hears him, if God even loves him anymore or if God is interested in ever helping him again. Then he vows to fill his mind with what is actually true; and having done that, he has a complete attitude reversal! He is overwhelmed with God's amazing power and willingness to act on behalf of His people! He knows God will address his needs.

He first realizes that his feelings are inconsistent with the truth, and he must force himself to think correctly. He must subjugate his mind and body to his will. Paul says in I Cor. 9:27, "I beat my body and make it my slave." Our bodies are our tools to help us live as God wants us to. They serve us, we do not serve them. At times we must take ourselves by the scruff of the neck and will ourselves to do what needs to be done.

So he causes himself to think about God's past actions: I WILL remember, I WILL consider, I WILL meditate... on God's amazing miracles and mighty deeds. He chooses one specific miracle to ponder, the parting of the Red Sea. He pictures the scenario in great detail; what it looked like, what it sounded like, what people experienced, what it felt like to BE there!

He ends up being completely overwhelmed with how incredible God's power is and to what ends God will go to to help and protect His people! He says in effect, "Is there anyone as totally incredible as our GOD?! Anyone so powerful and so willing to work on behalf of his people?"

He has moved from despair and hopelessness to awe. He is fully convinced that his God is vitally concerned with his people's needs and stands ready and willing to meet them!

Today, if your feelings are not consistent with truth as we know it from God's Word, WILL yourself to focus on what's true about Him and what He's done in the past and be amazed and encouraged!

Facilitated Prayer:

Find a location where you can focus your mind and calm your spirit as you move into a time of prayer. Spend the next few minutes using the P-R-A-Y prompts to enter into a conversation with God. The prompts are to help focus your time of prayer by taking the guesswork out of who and what to pray about each day.

·Day 40·

PRAY:

Praise	Take one minute to be encouraged by God's past work so you can praise Him in the present.
Repent	Take one minute to remember, consider, and meditate on what God has done and revealed to you in the past.
Ask for Others	Take two minutes to pray for those who need grace to "will" themselves toward trusting God with their future.
Your Needs	Take two minutes to consider your feelings that are not consistent with God's truth. "Will yourself" to focus on what's true about God from His Word.

Taking Notes:

_____

_____

_____

_____

_____

_____

_____

_____

_____

_____

_____

Psalm 82:1-8
Linda Owens | Edwardsville MetroGroup Leader

When I was a child I would cry out "THAT'S NOT FAIR!" THAT'S NOT FAIR!"

As a child, I expected everything to be fair. As an adult, I realized life wasn't about being fair. It was about doing what is right. My mom and dad taught me what was right and wrong in their eyes. As an adult, searching for God by reading the Bible and receiving Jesus as my Savior, I am learning what is right and wrong in God's eyes, not in mine or man's.

God is Judge over all the earth. God is Judge over all the judges and rulers of the earth. Here in Psalm 82, these judges are referred to as "gods". Although these rulers didn't necessarily follow the God of the Old Testament, He put them in place and gave them their position. When rulers don't seek God's direction, it is easy for them to become guilty of corruption and wrongdoing. Under their administration, the rich were often favored while the poor were oppressed. They didn't hold people accountable for their wrongs and didn't punish them either; so quite often the innocent suffered as a result of the evil. These evil rulers had been warned. However despite all the warnings, there was no change in their behavior. The results of their failure to act righteously and wisely caused the foundation of society to be unstable and law and order all but vanished. As a result, the psalmist calls out to God to rebuke them and judge them.

Like these evil rulers, when we do what is right in our own eyes and don't seek God's direction, we will also walk in the darkness of sin because we are mere humans. But as Christians who believe in Jesus, we are privileged to have God's Holy Spirit within us to guide us into Truth. As we read and believe God's Word, we share His Word and Truth with others.

Facilitated Prayer:

Find a location where you can focus your mind and calm your spirit as you move into a time of prayer. Spend the next few minutes using the P-R-A-Y prompts to enter into a conversation with God. The prompts are to help focus your time of prayer by taking the guesswork out of who and what to pray about each day.

·Day 41·

PRAY:

Praise	Take one minute to thank Him for being one God, judge, and ruler over all.
Repent	Take one minute to repent of situations in your life where you are doing "right in your own eyes" and not seeking God's direction.
Ask for Others	Take two minutes to pray for those who need to remember that one God and one Judge is truly trustworthy.
Your Needs	Take two minutes to pray about where you need God's wisdom and guidance in your life.

Taking Notes:

_____

_____

_____

_____

_____

_____

_____

_____

_____

_____

_____

Psalm 84:1-12

Kevin Rinkle | Edwardsville MetroGroup Leader

When I wake up in the morning, I am so happy that the first thing I see is my wife lying next to me in bed. I so enjoy our morning conversation and the look on her face as I tell her "I love you". However, my words and feelings do not hold a candle to the praise and worship offered to God by the author of Psalm 84.

My soul yearns, even faints, for the courts [house] of the LORD; my heart and my flesh cry out for the living God. (v2) The words of the psalm show a servant in clear adoration of his Master...LORD Almighty, my King and my God. (v3)

As much enjoyment and truth as there is in my morning ritual with my wife, how much more is there in our relationship with our glorious Father? Take a moment to feel the love of the psalmist. Feel the intention and fullness of his message. And feel the smile and warmth returned by God as He receives what you offer. All glory to our Father.

Facilitated Prayer:

Find a location where you can focus your mind and calm your spirit as you move into a time of prayer. Spend the next few minutes using the P-R-A-Y prompts to enter into a conversation with God. The prompts are to help focus your time of prayer by taking the guesswork out of who and what to pray about each day.

·Day 42·

PRAY:

Praise	Take one minute to express your joy and love for God your Father.
Repent	Take one minute to resolve in your heart to adore spending time with God.
Ask for Others	Take two minutes to pray for someone in your life that hasn't experienced the joy of knowing and loving God.
Your Needs	Take two minutes to pray about how you can continue cultivating a loving relationship with your heavenly Father.

Taking Notes:

_____

_____

_____

_____

_____

_____

_____

_____

_____

_____

_____

•Day 43•

Psalm 85:1-7
Jay Lowry | Vandalia MetroGroup Leader

Don't these verses sum up the typical human response to God? "God you've done all these amazing things in the past, but there are these present day things we're not sure you'll do."

So many times in my personal life I look at how insane the children of Israel were in their behavior. They repeatedly screwed up, over and over and over again. And God forgives and restores His relationship with them over and over and over again. It's like they can't see what they are doing. They see what has happened in the past; but when trouble strikes again, they forget how loving and forgiving God is when they repented in the past.

Aren't we the same today? We are ALL constantly messing up in the same ways. But when we go to God and seek forgiveness and repent, He is ALWAYS there to restore the relationship and forgive us. We need to look at the history of love God has shown us, be thankful for the forgiveness he consistently demonstrates, and seek to grow closer to Him.

Facilitated Prayer:

Find a location where you can focus your mind and calm your spirit as you move into a time of prayer. Spend the next few minutes using the P-R-A-Y prompts to enter into a conversation with God. The prompts are to help focus your time of prayer by taking the guesswork out of who and what to pray about each day.

·Day 43·

PRAY:

Praise	Take one minute to praise God for the amazing things He has done in your past.
Repent	Take one minute to be real with God about areas in your life where you keep messing up, and then seek His forgiveness.
Ask for Others	Take two minutes to pray for those who need the God of Grace to break the cycle of sin and struggle in their life.
Your Needs	Take two minutes to seek out a plan from God to keep you from messing up all over again and falling back into sin.

Taking Notes:

_____

_____

_____

_____

_____

_____

_____

_____

_____

_____

_____

·Day 44·

Psalm 85:8-13
Mike & Trudy Grimm | Edwardsville MetroGroup Leaders

People experience seasons in their life when there is great celebration and other times when there is great tribulation. There are times when God's people are faithful, yet other times when His people are sinful. Both of these modern examples are simply the cycles of human life. Similarly, God's people in the Old Testament experienced both great suffering and committed insufferable sins. In many cases, they experienced drought, famine, death, and war. There were cycles when they strayed from God then turned back to Him. They recognized their shortfalls, and they prayed for restoration. Importantly, during those times of hardship, they also prayed for forgiveness because they recognized their sinful nature.

Have you ever noticed your prayer life is best during the worst of times? Why is our human nature such that we grow closer to God during the "rough" times?

One important fun fact. Today's reading was written by the Sons of Korah - the father was a leader known for his rebellion against both God and Moses. As we read today, we recognize that Korah's descendants, in spite of their father's rebellion, wrote this portion of the Bible, inspired by God himself. What a great example of the infinite grace of God! It should give us all tremendous peace and comfort knowing we as sinners are also blessed by God's grace.

God promises to listen to the requests from his faithful servants. That means we not only need to communicate with God through our prayer lives, but we also need to listen to what God says. Said differently, we need to pray to God, be faithful according to His Word, then listen to what He says. The Lord promises to provide us with what is good (righteousness, grace, salvation etc) in these passages. He also promises us peace.

Let's collectively encourage Metro Community Church in our prayer life, talk and listen to God, and let's experience His promises of peace, love, faithfulness and grace as we live our lives together.

Facilitated Prayer:

Find a location where you can focus your mind and calm your spirit as you move into a time of prayer. Spend the next few minutes using the P-R-A-Y prompts to enter into a conversation with God. The prompts are to help focus your time of prayer by taking the guesswork out of who and what to pray about each day.

·Day 44·

PRAY:

Praise	Take one minute to praise God for being consistent despite us being so inconsistent in following Him.
Repent	Take one minute to access where you are in the "cycle of human life". Confess areas where you need to change or ask for God's forgiveness.
Ask for Others	Take two minutes to pray for anyone like a "Korah" in your life who is rebellious and against God.
Your Needs	Take two minutes to reflect again on the passage through prayer, seeking God for what is good (righteousness, grace, salvation, etc).

Taking Notes:

_____

_____

_____

_____

_____

_____

_____

_____

_____

_____

_____

Psalm 86:1-7
Dan & Amanda Riddle | Edwardsville MetroGroup Leaders

Have you felt like you are so small or that your personal issues are too insignificant to matter to God? Have you been scared or intimidated to ask God for the things you need or desire? You are not alone. In actuality, God desires to hear from you through prayer and he is capable of providing in our personal lives.

David's prayer in Psalm 86 is a wonderful example of just that. David humbly comes to God in prayer. David even starts the prayer by asking God to "Bend down" or "Incline Your ear". This shows that David feels that he as an individual matters to God. He is exalting and praising God while also asking God to provide him with mercy, joy, forgiveness and protection. David has a personal relationship with God and he knows God is capable of providing each of the things he asks God for. David is aware that he isn't capable of fully providing these things for himself, and he is fully relying on God.

No matter how small or insignificant you feel, God loves you and wants to have an open line of communication with you through prayer. This is true when times are good and in the challenging or troublesome times of your life.

Facilitated Prayer:

Find a location where you can focus your mind and calm your spirit as you move into a time of prayer. Spend the next few minutes using the P-R-A-Y prompts to enter into a conversation with God. The prompts are to help focus your time of prayer by taking the guesswork out of who and what to pray about each day.

·Day 45·

PRAY:

Praise	Take one minute to praise God for His personal relationship with you.
Repent	Take one minute to confess times of feeling small or insignificant.
Ask for Others	Take two minutes to pray for someone who feels unseen or unknown by God.
Your Needs	Take two minutes through prayer to examine where you need to trust God to provide mercy, joy, forgiveness and protection in your life.

Taking Notes:

_____

_____

_____

_____

_____

_____

_____

_____

_____

_____

_____

·Day 46·

Psalm 86:8-13
Bethany Horstmann | Edwardsville MetroGroup Leader

In our fast-paced world, there rarely seems time to pause. Our attention is divided from sunup to sundown. We live in a world of division, pain, and sin at every turn. It can feel overwhelming and hopeless. We can find comfort in knowing that God created it all and designed us to be in unity with others, bringing honor to him. The wonder we see in this world is created by God. When we slow down, we have a better perspective to see God's majesty.

Aligning ourselves with God requires us to be "doers" and not just receptacles of God's love and goodness. It's more than just, "What can He do for me?" We must ask ourselves, "What can I do for Him?" We are called to action! He uses us as He sees fit in every community in which he has placed us. We are placed in our schools, jobs, churches, organizations, neighborhoods, and communities for a reason. We can make a choice to step into action through our obedience and commitment to learn. He can make us into the people He wants us to be. We don't have to be well-qualified or equipped...just willing.

In turn, God's love is also an action! He cares for the things that matter to us. He delivered us from death. Our 'thank you' to Him is our praise, in moments of quiet solitude or public declarations. Have we taken a moment to pause and reflect on his greatness today?

Facilitated Prayer:

Find a location where you can focus your mind and calm your spirit as you move into a time of prayer. Spend the next few minutes using the P-R-A-Y prompts to enter into a conversation with God. The prompts are to help focus your time of prayer by taking the guesswork out of who and what to pray about each day.

·Day 46·

PRAY:

Praise	Take one minute to praise God for His greatness.
Repent	Take one minute to confess when you have become a "receptacle of God's love and goodness" and have failed to live out your faith with action.
Ask for Others	Take two minutes to pray for those who need to experience God's steadfast love.
Your Needs	Take two minutes to ask God "What can I do for You?". Let His Spirit lead you to a faith with action.

Taking Notes:

_____

_____

_____

_____

_____

_____

_____

_____

_____

_____

_____

·Day 47·

Psalm 90:1-8
Shannon McWhorter | Edwardsville MetroGroup Leader

Psalm 90 is the only psalm that was written by Moses; it is also the oldest psalm in the Book of Psalms. When Moses penned these words, he was leading the people of Israel through the wilderness. For generations and generations, the Israelites had been homeless -- first as slaves living in a land not belonging to them and then as nomads wandering in the desert because of their sin and disbelief. And yet Moses starts Psalm 90 by saying that God is their dwelling place, their refuge, their home; He is their safe place.

In addition, Moses goes on to say that even before the mountains were formed or the whole earth was created, God existed. He is not a god of stone created by human hands. He is the Creator of the world. He has always been. He will always be. As humans, we are frail, and our lives are short; we wither like the grass. Yet God is eternal and a thousand years in His presence will seem like but a day; He is everlasting to everlasting. This is why we can take refuge in him; He will always be there when we turn to Him.

We can take comfort in knowing and believing God is our refuge in our times of trouble. When we feel that we don't belong or we find ourselves aimlessly wandering through the desert times of life, God is our dwelling place. In God alone, we can find our everlasting refuge, our never-ending safe haven. We can run to him, like the prodigal son who ran to his father's open arms, knowing that He will always welcome us with His open arms. He will always be our dwelling place.

Facilitated Prayer:

Find a location where you can focus your mind and calm your spirit as you move into a time of prayer. Spend the next few minutes using the P-R-A-Y prompts to enter into a conversation with God. The prompts are to help focus your time of prayer by taking the guesswork out of who and what to pray about each day.

·Day 47·

PRAY:

Praise	Take one minute to thank God for being "our everlasting refuge, our never-ending safe haven."
Repent	Take one minute to confess how you have been like the prodigal son and need to run back to God the Father's open arms.
Ask for Others	Take two minutes to pray for those who are wandering in a spiritual wilderness in need of an eternal dwelling place.
Your Needs	Take two minutes to pray about finding God as your dwelling place concerning matters that are troubling your heart this week.

Taking Notes:

_____

_____

_____

_____

_____

_____

_____

_____

_____

_____

_____

·Day 48·

Psalm 90:9-17
Ethan Jones | Vandalia MetroGroup Leader

When reading this passage, you can see two extremes...misery and hope. Misery in the fact that this life is filled with pain and trouble as it says in verse 10. This passage hits home on the brevity of life, and true restoration from trouble comes only from the Lord. My Bible describes this psalm as 'a prayer of Moses, the man of God.' As followers of God, it's no surprise to us that troubles still come to us. We see this in the lives of those in Scripture, and we even see trouble come to the life of our Savior, Jesus Christ. In school our professor asked the class, "If we were going to follow a suffering messiah, then how could we expect our lives to be any different?" As God's children we accept that trouble will come, yet Jesus also taught us where our hope comes from in our times of trouble. He never stopped following God. Jesus taught us to trust our Heavenly Father.

When we look at this psalm, we can see that same message. Verses 15-17 call for gladness to replace our former misery, for God's servants to see Him work, for our children to see His glory, and for God to show us His approval. In this life it is so easy to get caught up in the negative and to feel distant from God. As you read this psalm, I pray you are filled with hope; and God shows you that even though trouble surrounds us, He is still in control.

I love this acronym for the word hope...Hold On, Pain Ends. That is a great focus to have in our relationship with God; not dwelling on what is, but what will be. The beginning of this passage is filled with what could be seen as darkness, but it is quickly turned to hope and begging God to come into the situation. Let that be our prayer...turn darkness to light.

Facilitated Prayer:

Find a location where you can focus your mind and calm your spirit as you move into a time of prayer. Spend the next few minutes using the P-R-A-Y prompts to enter into a conversation with God. The prompts are to help focus your time of prayer by taking the guesswork out of who and what to pray about each day.

·Day 48·

PRAY:

Praise	Take one minute of gratitude for how valuable God's wisdom has been for you over the years.
Repent	Take one minute to admit where you have lost sight of hope in God.
Ask for Others	Take two minutes to pray for those who need to see and know that God is at work in and through difficult days
Your Needs	Take two minutes to pray about how you will Hold On [until] Pain Ends. Let God turn your "darkness to light".

Taking Notes:

_____

_____

_____

_____

_____

_____

_____

_____

_____

_____

_____

·Day 49·

Psalm 91:1-10
Julie Mead | Edwardsville MetroGroup Leader

What comes to mind when you read the introductory verses of this passage? It's not difficult to visualize the metaphorical wings and feathers of a magnificent bald eagle. With an average wingspan of 6.7 feet, it's no wonder that this great bird's wings are each fitted with inner feathers as long as 14 inches and outer feathers of nearly 2 feet. A mature adult has around 7,200 feathers in total. These attributes enable it to fly at 10,000 to 20,000 feet at 35 to 40 miles an hour.

Whether it is an eagle, a hen, or any other type of bird, the verses illustrate the protection, the security, and the refuge of our loving God. To cast a shadow implies nearness. As we dwell in His shelter, He is as near as a parent bird to its young in the nest. Some feathers insulate. Others on the wing are composed of tiny barbs that enable the resistance of water and air to not only enable flight but also shield from the elements and offer refuge from potential harm. The psalm is an illustration of how we can rest assured, knowing we are protected and secure in God's trustworthiness, faithfulness, and limitless love.

To fully experience the promise of God's provision and protection, we must commit to pray. Prayer, whether a petition or praise, brings us near to God and conveys the kind of dependence and trust that a baby bird has for its parent. Prayer protects our minds and hearts from the negative effects of difficulties in our lives. It is a shield against fear. Also as we pray for others, it encourages empathy, compassion and helps us become others-focused. Like an eagle in flight, prayer carries away our burdens, lifts our praises, and soars to our Heavenly Father.

Facilitated Prayer:

Find a location where you can focus your mind and calm your spirit as you move into a time of prayer. Spend the next few minutes using the P-R-A-Y prompts to enter into a conversation with God. The prompts are to help focus your time of prayer by taking the guesswork out of who and what to pray about each day.

·Day 49·

PRAY:

Praise	Take one minute to thank God for being near to us and offering us a place of security and protection.
Repent	Take one minute to confess when you have stepped outside of God's provision of protection in your life.
Ask for Others	Take two minutes to pray for those in your life that are in desperate need of God's shield of protection.
Your Needs	Take two minutes to dwell in God's shelter through prayer. Ask God to protect your mind and heart from the negative effects of the difficulties in your life.

Taking Notes:

_____

_____

_____

_____

_____

_____

_____

_____

_____

_____

_____

Psalm 94:12-23
Annie Pense| Edwardsville MetroGroup Leader

I don't know about you, but I can say for myself that I am not always joyful when I am disciplined. I wasn't joyful about it as a child and I'm not always joyful as an adult. When you read this verse you may think of joy as happy. However, joy doesn't always mean happiness. Happiness is an emotion. Joy is deeper! True joy comes from God.

As I have matured and my relationship with God has grown and deepened, my acceptance of discipline has improved. Along with my acceptance of the discipline, I am also able to find joy in it. Through many of life's challenges I have learned that I can and I do trust God. So if I trust Him, I can trust that the discipline I may receive is for my own good and by receiving it, it only brings me closer to Him. He's not out to harm me but to keep me safe. His discipline acts as guard rails that are in place for my safety. He is teaching me and molding me so I can display more of His character.

The beauty in it all is that for those of us who love God and have a relationship with Him, rest will come after the affliction. I encourage you to trust in Him. Find joy (peace) in Him. Rest in peace... peace in knowing that the discipline is there not just any reason, but a good reason.

God, thank you for loving me so much that you don't give up on me. Thank you that you love me enough that you want to teach me and have a good and healthy relationship with me. Help me, God, to find peace and joy and rest in my times of discipline. God help me to learn and be more like you.

Facilitated Prayer:

Find a location where you can focus your mind and calm your spirit as you move into a time of prayer. Spend the next few minutes using the P-R-A-Y prompts to enter into a conversation with God. The prompts are to help focus your time of prayer by taking the guesswork out of who and what to pray about each day.

·Day 50·

PRAY:

Praise	Take one minute to thank God for not giving up on you.
Repent	Take one minute to confess a time when you have grumbled over God's discipline
Ask for Others	Take two minutes to pray for those who you know that need to experience God's joy and rest through times of godly discipline.
Your Needs	Take two minutes to reflect on God's discipline in your life and that He would reveal to you guard rails that will allow you to keep growing in Him.

Taking Notes:

_____

_____

_____

_____

_____

_____

_____

_____

_____

_____

Psalm 95:1-7
Brad Rickert| Edwardsville MetroGroup Leader

How often do you pause to contemplate and appreciate all that you possess? Most of us have a comfortable bed where we slept last night sheltered by the roof over our homes. We wake up, take warm showers, dress ourselves, and prepare breakfast for our families. We have cars to drive us to our jobs, where we earn money to support our needs. However, amidst the familiarity of these blessings, do we truly take the time to reflect on their significance and the reasons behind their presence in our lives?

Psalm 95 sheds light on the reasons. David alludes to God as the "great King above all Gods" and the "rock of our salvation." The "why" behind all that we have is rooted in God's love for us. As Pastor Seth mentioned recently in his message series, "Appellations", JEHOVAH-JIREH translates to "The Lord Will Provide." God provides for us because we have a higher calling and a purpose to fulfill. God has done all the work. He holds the depths of the earth and the mightiest mountains in His hands. He is the Creator of the seas and the land. So, what can we do to give glory to God for His countless blessings upon us?

Throughout Scripture, we find numerous instances of groups of people, like the Israelites, who would often fail to remember and reflect upon the identity of the one true Creator of all things. While we may not worship golden calves, if we fail to give God the glory in everything we do, to whom are we attributing that glory? In Psalm 95, David employs the phrase "Come, let us" as an invitational reminder to praise, sing, and express thanksgiving to the Creator. We accept this invitation and offer our praise to God through prayer. It is during prayer that we can intimately connect with God, growing in our relationship with Him and giving Him the praise He truly deserves.

My "circle" is completed daily as I listen to the Bible on my way to work, followed by a dedicated prayer time before I step out of my car. During this uninterrupted time, I thank and praise God for all He has provided, including my car, my job, my church family, my Christ-centered friends, and more. When is your dedicated daily prayer time? Are you intentionally setting aside time to prioritize God? The more we express daily gratitude in our prayers, the more it will daily manifest in our interactions with others.

Facilitated Prayer:

Find a location where you can focus your mind and calm your spirit as you move into a time of prayer. Spend the next few minutes using the P-R-A-Y prompts to enter into a conversation with God. The prompts are to help focus your time of prayer by taking the guesswork out of who and what to pray about each day.

·Day 51·

PRAY:

Praise	Take one minute to count your blessings for everything God has provided you!!
Repent	Take one minute to admit times where you have been unthankful.
Ask for Others	Take two minutes to pray about how you can share something God has given you to bless someone else.
Your Needs	Take two minutes to seek God through prayer on how you should prioritize your time. Pray that you would be dedicated to spending time with Him daily.

Taking Notes:

_____

_____

_____

_____

_____

_____

_____

_____

_____

_____

_____

·Day 52·

Psalm 99:1-9
Laraeli Barron | MetroCollege Group Leader

What words do you think of when you reflect on God's character? Does the word "loving" come to mind, maybe merciful, or powerful? If we are being honest, sometimes we tend to think of God more as restrictive and judgmental; and if we are being very honest, some of us might admit we don't ever really think of God and His character at all! While God truly is full of grace and abounding in love, the perfect word to describe God is "holy". This is not an opinion; in fact, the Bible uses "holy" to describe God's character more than any other adjective.

Holiness is not a concept we humans grasp effortlessly. The reality is unless you encounter the living God, you will not have any understanding of what "holy" truly means. As 1 Samuel 2:2 tells us, "There is no one Holy like the LORD." In the face of this truth, we must recognize all the preconceived judgments we attach to God when examined in the light of His holiness.

Instead of letting His Word sink in (that because He is Holy, we are called toward reverence and awe), we assume that God's holiness demands our own great accomplishments in His name. We fall into the trap of a performance-based faith, and we water down the wonder of God's perfection and power by striving to attain perfection and gain power for ourselves. The reality is God's holiness is on display by the way He refines our hearts and inclines our souls toward His love by His own might.

The proper response to encountering the Holy God is not working toward holiness in our own strength but pausing and praising God in His holy presence, which changes our hearts and desires. Although God is holy and reigning in glory for eternity, He is not sticking up his perfect nose at us when we crash and burn...again. He is beckoning us to sit and catch up with the reality that the God of angel armies is inviting us to exalt His name with our imperfect lips.

Facilitated Prayer:

Find a location where you can focus your mind and calm your spirit as you move into a time of prayer. Spend the next few minutes using the P-R-A-Y prompts to enter into a conversation with God. The prompts are to help focus your time of prayer by taking the guesswork out of who and what to pray about each day.

·Day 52·

PRAY:

Praise	Take one minute to be in reverence and awe of God's holiness!
Repent	Take one minute to confess times when you have assumed that God's holiness demands your own great accomplishments in His name.
Ask for Others	Take two minutes to pray for those who need to know that God's holiness allows Him to purify their hearts.
Your Needs	Take two minutes to pray about how God's holiness will impact your desires and conduct this week.

Taking Notes:

_____

_____

_____

_____

_____

_____

_____

_____

_____

_____

_____

·Day 53·

Psalm 100:1-5
James Ford | Edwardsville MetroGroup Leader

Be thankful. That is the message that we are instructed to do in this psalm. Simple, straightforward. Give thanks. Yet, there are many times in my own life where I need to be told to do this. I need to read this and be reminded to give thanks to God! Life has a way of knocking each one of us down at different points. Examples could include general busyness of life where you feel like you are constantly struggling to keep up, a family issue, a relational struggle, a problem with your job, or an unexpected health problem. So many things can happen to distract us from giving thanks to God.

Reading something like this Psalm is an instant reminder for myself to focus on the things that I can be thankful of regardless of the situations I'm currently facing. I find comfort and peace that God doesn't change regardless of the situation I'm facing. He is the only constant in my life. No matter what is going on I am thankful that God loves me. I will be thankful "for the Lord is good, and his faithful love endures forever." Psalms 100:5a

After reading this passage and praying, it may be helpful to write down things that you are thankful for in your life. This exercise has helped me refocus on the good things God has done and will continue to do in my life. There are so many things to thank God for!

Facilitated Prayer:

Find a location where you can focus your mind and calm your spirit as you move into a time of prayer. Spend the next few minutes using the P-R-A-Y prompts to enter into a conversation with God. The prompts are to help focus your time of prayer by taking the guesswork out of who and what to pray about each day.

·Day 53·

PRAY:

Praise	Take one minute to praise God today for His enduring love and His faithfulness to all generations.
Repent	Take one minute to repent of any attitudes of ungratefulness in your life.
Ask for Others	Take two minutes to pray for family or friends that are being knocked down by the pressures of life.
Your Needs	Take two minutes to pray for opportunities to serve the Lord with gladness.

Taking Notes:

_____

_____

_____

_____

_____

_____

_____

_____

_____

_____

Psalm 100:1-5
Emileigh Ziebka | Edwardsville MetroGroup Leader

Verse 2: Your home, your family, is one of the greatest ministries the Lord will call you to, but it can be challenging with family members more easily taken for granted and where you are more comfortable with your emotions. Be in prayer. God will help you overcome this challenge and be a model of integrity to your kids, grandkids, spouse, those with whom you live.

What about outside your home? In 2 Samuel 20, we read of a "wise woman" who bravely spoke up for her city and whose counsel saved her city from destruction. She had developed a reputation of wisdom, one to be trusted. Pray the Lord will guide you to develop a reputation of integrity with your neighbors, coworkers, and community. When you are a person of integrity, you can be trusted inside and outside your home.

Verses 3-4: David vowed not to let anything worthless guide him. Proverbs 13:20 advises us to walk with the wise and become wise. We ought to walk with those of integrity so we also will become a person of integrity. You will inevitably become like those with whom you invest the most time; therefore, be wise about who and what guides your heart. Pray that the Lord will guide you to others who live with integrity.

Verses 5-8: King David vowed to be intentional about who he surrounded himself with. This call goes deeper than protecting our sense of integrity when choosing our inner circle. These verses prompt a call to pray for your leaders. We must pray that our leaders in the church and government will value this level of intention and influence.

Facilitated Prayer:

Find a location where you can focus your mind and calm your spirit as you move into a time of prayer. Spend the next few minutes using the P-R-A-Y prompts to enter into a conversation with God. The prompts are to help focus your time of prayer by taking the guesswork out of who and what to pray about each day.

·Day 54·

PRAY:

Praise	Take one minute to thank God for people of integrity God has used to impact your life.
Repent	Take one minute to confess any area of your life that is not defined by being a person of integrity.
Ask for Others	Take two minutes to pray for your church and government leaders.
Your Needs	Take two minutes to pray that the Lord will guide you to others who live with integrity so that you can experience authentic community.

Taking Notes:

_____

_____

_____

_____

_____

_____

_____

_____

_____

_____

_____

·Day 55·

Psalm 103:1-12
Mati Barron | Metro Communications Team

Do you ever find yourself questioning if God really has forgiven your sin? At face value, of course we all know the answer to this...if we have accepted Jesus' sacrifice, yes of course we are forgiven! But often, although our mouths proclaim our clean slate with God, our hearts and minds are far from actually believing our sin could ever be removed from us.

This idea that God "kind of" forgives your sin shows up in small ways. Maybe you discredit yourself and refuse to believe God could use someone like you to do His work. Maybe you reject good gifts God sends your way because you don't feel worthy. Maybe deep down, your obedience to God is in fear that you're on thin ice with Him because of a murky past. Wherever you find yourself, if you think God looks at you and sees anything less than the righteousness of Jesus, it's time to inspect and correct the way you're thinking!

Psalm 103:10 makes a bold statement...God does not deal with us according to our sins. Let that sink in for a moment. Despite what we should receive as punishment for our sin, in Christ, God doesn't deal with us according to that or repay us for our evil. It goes on to say, "as far as the east is from the west, so far does he remove our transgressions from us," (Psalm 103:12).

Can you imagine a life where you lived knowing your sin had truly been removed from you, as far as the earth stretches east to west? Our God loves us with a faithful steadfast love. It is His joy to remove our transgressions from us through His Son Jesus! And once we have that assurance of forgiveness, living life knowing that God sees the blood of Jesus and not your sin when He looks at you, gives us encouragement to toss away our old thinking patterns of regretting the past or not feeling good enough to be used by God.

Today, reflect on sin you may need to repent of. Maybe you've been punishing yourself for sin God has already forgiven! Seek the heart of the Lord as you spend time with Him today and ask Him to show you if there are any areas in your life that He wants you to surrender, so He can redeem them even more.

Facilitated Prayer:

Find a location where you can focus your mind and calm your spirit as you move into a time of prayer. Spend the next few minutes using the P-R-A-Y prompts to enter into a conversation with God. The prompts are to help focus your time of prayer by taking the guesswork out of who and what to pray about each day.

·Day 55·

PRAY:

Praise	Take one minute to praise God today for His steadfast love and His neverending forgiveness
Repent	Take one minute to reflect on any sin you need to repent of.
Ask for Others	Take two minutes to pray for someone you know who struggles with feeling unworthy in regards to their faith
Your Needs	Take two minutes to share with God an area or two where you struggle with feeling inadequate.

Taking Notes:

_____

_____

_____

_____

_____

_____

_____

_____

_____

_____

·Day 56·

Psalm 106:1-5
Matt Warren | Edwardsville MetroGroup Leader

I will praise you, Lord! When I pray, I always start my prayer with a "thank you" to God. Thank you for my health, my family, my church, my community, etc. I should be starting my prayer with PRAISE! A celebration of all those things I am thankful for; of which, I am not worthy. Even though I am not worthy, God still blesses me daily. He blesses all those who follow Him.

I am often thankful for the blessings I am aware of in my life. He has provided many more blessings and gifts of which I am unaware. He gives and gives and gives! He gives so much that I cannot fully comprehend His grace. By choosing a path to follow Him, I have been given so much I do not deserve! We are in His favor when we show others His love through our words and actions. And when I do recognize and realize His awe-inspiring blessings, I should celebrate by praising Him.

The unconditional love He has provided to each and every one of us is undeserved, but His grace and love is still given to us daily. We simply cannot comprehend the magnitude of these gifts. We often fall short with our families, our friends, and our relationship with God, but He still loves us and we should celebrate God's presence and power in our lives.

We are sinful people who do not deserve the blessings and gifts from God: but by following Him, we receive His grace, His love, and redemption. These are the greatest gifts of all and we should celebrate Him!

Facilitated Prayer:

Find a location where you can focus your mind and calm your spirit as you move into a time of prayer. Spend the next few minutes using the P-R-A-Y prompts to enter into a conversation with God. The prompts are to help focus your time of prayer by taking the guesswork out of who and what to pray about each day.

·Day 56·

PRAY:

Praise	Take one minute to praise God for His unconditional love for you.
Repent	Take one minute to reflect and repent of your own unworthiness.
Ask for Others	Take two minutes to pray for neighbors and co-workers who need to know the reason you celebrate a risen and ministering Savior.
Your Needs	Take two minutes to commit through prayer to keep following Jesus so you can experience His grace, His love, and His continued redemptive work in your life

Taking Notes:

_____

_____

_____

_____

_____

_____

_____

_____

_____

_____

_____

•Day 57•

Psalm 109:21-28 | Refuge in the Ridicule
Tim Weihrauch | Vandalia Campus Pastor

Have you ever been ridiculed? It may have shown up as "innocent teasing" or maybe it was as obvious as a bully waiting for you after school. There tends to be a natural progression of how this affects us, and we find that progression in Psalm 109. Early on, we put on a brave front and act like it doesn't affect us at all. Then, the jabs go inward and start penetrating the depths of our heart. It begins to change how we think until we become desperate to find a way out. Every day, we hesitate to get out of bed, because we aren't sure we can face it again. Days move slowly, and it feels as though it could be our breaking point.

This is the struggle of David within this Psalm. Whether it was the Philistines, King Saul or his own son, he understood the ridicule that comes from those who desire to see the people of God (Jehovah -first Lord in v. 21; Adonai - second Lord in v. 21) falter, fail and fade away. His response was to pray and fast which only added to the ridicule, because they could see his physical features fading with his inner strength. He became desperate for the refuge that only Jehovah Elohim can provide.

Hebrews 5:7-10 lets us see that Jesus also walked this path and received refuge from His Father. Our refuge will be ultimately realized in eternity, but we have a High Priest that is ready to give grace and mercy as we approach His throne in our time of need (Heb. 4:15-16).

Spend time in prayer for those who may be walking through ridicule for their faith in Jesus. This may be ridicule that we observe someone we know experiencing or it may be those around the world who we will not know until eternity that are experiencing ridicule and persecution for their faith. Pray for their inner strength in Christ to be renewed. Pray that they would see God's help, salvation and faithful love. Pray that those who ridicule might come to an understanding of the salvation they currently mock; so they too may truly find a refuge for their souls.

Facilitated Prayer:

Find a location where you can focus your mind and calm your spirit as you move into a time of prayer. Spend the next few minutes using the P-R-A-Y prompts to enter into a conversation with God. The prompts are to help focus your time of prayer by taking the guesswork out of who and what to pray about each day.

·Day 57·

PRAY:

Praise	Take one minute to praise God for being your refuge in times of ridicule.
Repent	Take one minute to repent of times you failed to turn to God when you were ridiculed.
Ask for Others	Take two minutes to pray for those around the world who are ridiculed for their faith in God.
Your Needs	Take two minutes to ask God for his grace and mercy as you turn to Him as your refuge.

Taking Notes:

_____

_____

_____

_____

_____

_____

_____

_____

_____

_____

_____

·Day 58·

Psalm 112:1-10
Steve Thimpson | Edwardsville MetroGroup Leader

How many times have we heard that children should obey their parents? How many times have we heard that we should obey the law? How many times do we listen to the wise counsel of others and then live our lives accordingly? How many times do we follow rules or guidelines that will better our lives? Do you obey God's commands? God says in Psalm 112 that we will be blessed if we obey His commands.

This psalm is almost entirely dedicated to explaining the true characteristics of the believer in Jesus and the hope that we experience by obeying His commands. Some of the blessings mentioned in this chapter if we obey Him are: he fears the Lord, he delights in God's commandments, his descendants will be mighty on earth, he will have wealth and riches, he is gracious, he is full of compassion, he guides his affairs with discretion, he will never be shaken he will not be afraid of evil, he trusts in the Lord. That is quite an impressive list!

God loves to bless those who follow Him. We will all make mistakes in our lifetime but we should still see God developing His character in us while we live for Him. We will never be perfect but there should be signs of continued growth in Him as we obey His commands.

I know that I fall way short of the perfect being that Christ is. I will continue to pray for God's guidance. I pray that God will develop a more obedient me. I will strive to be more like Him.

Facilitated Prayer:

Find a location where you can focus your mind and calm your spirit as you move into a time of prayer. Spend the next few minutes using the P-R-A-Y prompts to enter into a conversation with God. The prompts are to help focus your time of prayer by taking the guesswork out of who and what to pray about each day.

·Day 58·

PRAY:

Praise	Take one minute to praise God for the blessings you have as a believer.
Repent	Take one minute to confess times you fall short in your obedience to His commands
Ask for Others	Take two minutes to pray for someone you know who has not turned their life over to Christ.
Your Needs	Take two minutes to ask God to help you delight in His Word.

Taking Notes:

_____

_____

_____

_____

_____

_____

_____

_____

_____

_____

·Day 59·

Psalm 114:1-8
Aaron Karlas | Edwardsville MetroGroup Leader

Am I really thankful for all God has provided for me? Do I tell him?

As a Dad I love providing for my kids. I love to buy them stuff, do things for them, spend time with them, teach them...I don't do it for their reaction, but it does matter to me. If they don't say anything or they say something totally unthankful, it hurts. When they say things like, "I wish I could have 'fill in the blank' like my friend, it's not fair", it is hard to take. However, when I provide my kids something and they hug me and say "Dad, I love you; thank you so much; you are the best Dad in the world", that is one of the best feelings in the world. Why do I think this is any different for God, who has provided me with so much more than I do for my kids? He gave His only Son to be tortured and sacrificed to take the punishment for my selfishness and save me from Eternal Hell. Doesn't it make sense that I would thank him every chance I get? When I sincerely thank him and tell him I love him, in prayer, I know it makes Him smile.

As a Christian in today's world, is it hard to talk about miracles of God? Do we worry that people, even Christians, will think we are "out-there", or "radical"? Do we worry that if we share a miracle that God has done in our life, it will sound like bragging? If God called me to post it on FaceBook, would I fear people's reaction? I have often not shared amazing things God has done in my life for these reasons. I think we need to share these things at God's prompting and timing. One way to know the timing and make sure it's not about us looking good, is to pray. Praying to God helps us remember to give him the credit and direct our timing. God still does miracles to show His Greatness and Christians should not be afraid to share this!

Facilitated Prayer:

Find a location where you can focus your mind and calm your spirit as you move into a time of prayer. Spend the next few minutes using the P-R-A-Y prompts to enter into a conversation with God. The prompts are to help focus your time of prayer by taking the guesswork out of who and what to pray about each day.

·Day 59·

As you "P-R-A-Y..."

PRAY:

Praise	Take a minute to praise God for the mighty works He has done in your life.
Repent	Take a minute to repent of a time when you had an ungrateful heart.
Ask for Others	Take two minutes to pray for those who need to see God's miraculous works in their life.
Your Needs	Take two minutes to ask God to reveal more of Himself to you.

Taking Notes:

_____

_____

_____

_____

_____

_____

_____

_____

_____

_____

·Day 60·

Psalm 116:1-7
Jill Klein | Edwardsville MetroGroup Leader

In all honesty, there are moments in my own personal faith journey when I question whether God is listening to my prayers, –moments when the feeling of His presence is absent, and moments when the question, "God where are you?" swirls through my mind. I think most of us reading this can say that we have experienced similar seasons in our walk with the Lord.

In those seasons of dryness, I try to enter a mode of reflection, remembering when God felt so close as I hit my knees in desperation. Those were moments when the evidence of His goodness was all around me as He mercifully answered my prayers through His provision, healing power, or the performance of any other miraculous work that only He is capable of.

When I read these seven verses the psalmist wrote, I instantly flip through my scrapbook of life and land on a couple key events where these words resonate. For example, the psalmist uses the word "death" in verse 3: "Death wrapped its ropes around me; the terrors of the grave overtook me. I saw only trouble and sorrow." I am not sure I can relate to the depth of the word "death" here, but I can relate to the fearful feeling that filled my soul in past seasons of life – the season of my parent's divorce, the season when anxiety overwhelmed me while competing in collegiate athletics, or even the season of transition as I prepared to graduate college but was still without a job offer.

It is that feeling of fear that humbles us and leads us to full reliance and dependence on God knowing He has already written our story to completion yet desiring a sense of peace and comfort within the storm. In those moments we draw closer, we pray with expectancy, because we are desperate for an answer; and the feeling of His presence is real and raw. Just like the psalmist writes - "Please, Lord save me!" - it becomes our battle cry. And in His timing, He answers. In His rich mercy, He bends down from above to meet us where we are and walks us to the other side. He reveals His goodness and saves us. He brings rest to our soul.

And after reflecting on the Lord's goodness in those moments, my heart moves back to praise in those seasons of dryness. Even if all we feel is the absence of His presence, He is still worthy to be praised through our prayer life. We need to continue to hit our knees, bow with reverence, and talk to God with praise on our tongue. He is there, He is listening, and above all - He is good.

·Day 60·

Facilitated Prayer:

Find a location where you can focus your mind and calm your spirit as you move into a time of prayer. Spend the next few minutes using the P-R-A-Y prompts to enter into a conversation with God. The prompts are to help focus your time of prayer by taking the guesswork out of who and what to pray about each day.

As you "P-R-A-Y..."

PRAY:

Praise	Take one minute to praise the Lord for knowing and hearing your voice through prayer.
Repent	Take one minute to think about the "scrapbook of your life". Turn over those pages that are defined by fear, overwhelmingness, and sorrow and give them to God.
Ask for Others	Take two minutes to pray for those who need "20/20 hindsight" to recall how God clearly proved He is faithful.
Your Needs	Take two minutes to humble yourself before God and ask Him to keep you walking in utter dependence on Him alone!

Taking Notes:

_____

_____

_____

_____

_____

_____

•Day 61•

Psalm 116:8-19
Michael Klein | Edwardsville MetroGroup Leader

There have been moments in my life that it felt like everything was crashing around me. There was a time when my dad was struggling with both physical and mental health issues, my parents were no longer living in the same house, my sister had moved across the country, and I felt like I was the one trying to hold it all together. I'm sure that you have experienced similar seasons in your life where it feels like things are out of control. This was also the case for the psalmist.

It was during this season of anxiety and desperation that I found myself most drawn to spending time in prayer and speaking with God. If I believe that God is good, that He truly wants what is best for me and that He hears my prayers, then what other option do I have than to pray to Him? The psalmist writes in verse 10, "I believed in you, so I said "I am deeply troubled, Lord."". It is BECAUSE the psalmist believed in Him and what God was capable of doing that the psalmist came to Him in prayer to express his troubles.

Hebrews 4:16 says, "Let us then approach God's throne of grace with confidence, so that we may receive mercy and find grace to help us in our time of need." This may not always mean the situation will be resolved as we want it to, but it will put us in a posture of reliance on Him and knowing He has the situation under control regardless of the outcome. That help in our time of need might be the healing we are looking for or it might be peace we need in the situation.

Whether we are in a time of desperation or in what might feel like the monotonous day-to-day grind, God wants us to approach Him in prayer with confidence and joy. The psalmist writes in verse 12, "What can I offer the Lord for all he has done for me?" He answers his own question in the following verses by saying multiple times he will "call on the name of the Lord." Prayer is a way we can thank God for all that He has done for us and worship Him. He loves us and wants to hear from us about both the big and small things happening in our lives.

Facilitated Prayer:

Find a location where you can focus your mind and calm your spirit as you move into a time of prayer. Spend the next few minutes using the P-R-A-Y prompts to enter into a conversation with God. The prompts are to help focus your time of prayer by taking the guesswork out of who and what to pray about each day.

·Day 61·

PRAY:

Praise	Take a minute to praise God for all that He has delivered you from.
Repent	Take a minute to repent of a time when you took matters in your own hands instead of turning to God.
Ask for Others	Take two minutes to pray for those you know who need to "call on the name of the Lord" (v 13).
Your Needs	Take two minutes to offer up thanksgiving and to call on the name of the Lord (v 17).

Taking Notes:

_____

_____

_____

_____

_____

_____

_____

_____

·Day 62·

Psalm 118:1-7
Jonny Sones | Edwardsville MetroGroup Leader

So many times we say God is good to us and we praise Him for that, but can we say that all the time? Do we praise God in the times of trials and tribulations or do we only praise Him when He answers our prayers? Do we rely on our own strength and understanding during our trials?

As you look into your heart can you honestly say I praise God because He is God, or do I praise Him because He gives me what I want. Our circumstances should change how we see and worship God.

God wants us to praise him because he is God and He is wholeheartedly 100% good. Praise Him in the good times and the bad, simply because He is God.

Please take a minute, pray, and examine your heart and really praise God. Praise Him for who He is, God!

Facilitated Prayer:

Find a location where you can focus your mind and calm your spirit as you move into a time of prayer. Spend the next few minutes using the P-R-A-Y prompts to enter into a conversation with God. The prompts are to help focus your time of prayer by taking the guesswork out of who and what to pray about each day.

·Day 62·

PRAY:

Praise	Take one minute to praise Him for who He is...God!
Repent	Take one minute to repent of only praising God when we get what we want.
Ask for Others	Take two minutes to pray for those who are experiencing hardships, that they could still praise God during their trials and tribulations.
Your Needs	Take two minutes to pray for whatever difficulties you are facing and express that God is still good and praiseworthy.

Taking Notes:

_____

_____

_____

_____

_____

_____

_____

_____

·Day 63·

Psalm 118:8-16
Mike Rumsey | Edwardsville MetroGroup Leader

Where do I go for refuge from a vortex of worldly voices and vices? Where do I go for wise counsel? Where do I go for reassurance of God's presence and provisions? Where do I go when I need to know God loves me, hears me, and will answer my prayers?

Let's go to the "heart" of Scripture. Psalm 118:8 marks the "textual center-point" within the sixty-six books of the Bible and reminds us that God remains our refuge from peers and politicians whose voices or vices may distract us from God's presence and provisions. David models the benefits of "20/20 hindsight". He lists several instances when he saw his faith and trust tested by dire circumstances and then he acknowledges how God countered each threat and answered David's prayers in the midst of each crisis.

So why is it that I can read this Psalm, stop to pray, and still struggle to find and feel refuge? In his book, The Necessity of Prayer, E.M. Bounds clarifies how faith & trust complete our act of praying: "Faith gives [prayer] color and tone, shapes its character, and secures its results. Trust is faith-be-come-absolute, ratified, consummated. There is, when all is said and done, a sort of venture in faith and its exercise. But trust is firm belief, it is faith in full flower."

As we read Psalm 118: 8-18 today, we see & hear how God provides refuge to those who fuel their prayers with faith & trust. E.M. Bounds goes on to say:

"Trust sees God doing things here and now.. Even more, prayer rises to a lofty eminence, and looking into the invisible and the eternal, realizes that God has done things and regards them as being already done. Trust brings eternity into the annals and happenings of time, transmutes the substance of hope into the reality of fruition, and changes promise into present possession."

God's eternal refuge becomes our present reality!

Facilitated Prayer:

Find a location where you can focus your mind and calm your spirit as you move into a time of prayer. Spend the next few minutes using the P-R-A-Y prompts to enter into a conversation with God. The prompts are to help focus your time of prayer by taking the guesswork out of who and what to pray about each day.

·Day 63·

PRAY:

Praise	Take one minute to praise God for being a "refuge" in this world.
Repent	Take one minute to confess any distractions in your life that keep you from finding true refuge in God.
Ask for Others	Take two minutes to pray for those who need to find the authentic refuge only God can provide.
Your Needs	Take two minutes to seek refuge and find God's presence & power through prayer.

Taking Notes:

_____

_____

_____

_____

_____

_____

_____

_____

·Day 64·

Psalm 118:23-29

Cristy Munro | Edwardsville MetroGroup Leader

WHAT? WAIT! WHAT? Can you see it? Can you hear that? Do you get it? Does it make any sense how this happened? Why the heck did it happen?

When the Lord acts or moves, do we really know anything at the time? In hindsight, do we really fully understand how it all came to pass, even when looking back? No. Our knowledge is finite; we cannot fully comprehend it all.

His works…His wonders are amazing!!! Each day is yet another point in time to witness how wonderful God is.

I didn't make this day, and I don't believe another human did either. I don't believe the intricacies of man evolved from an amoeba crawling out of mud, nor did man evolve from an ape. And the Milky Way didn't happen because of an explosion. The air that we breathe has a perfect mixture of elements in it, and if these percentages were minutely incorrect we would die…This just happened to have happened? There's no way!

I choose to believe that a Creator I call God made it all, and this amazing, infinite, omnipotent, omnipresent, and omniscient Creator made me. Why did he place me in this specific moment in time? Clueless. But He knows. Even clueless, I still have the ability to choose happiness, to rejoice in-and-about Him, and to be thankful for this moment in time.

Hey, wait yet another minute…because of my relationship with this ultimate Creator, I can take my concerns, my needs, my questions, my doubts to him? With praise, I can tie them to His altar, leave them there, and He will answer? Yes and yes!

Oh…..abundant praise and thanksgiving to you Lord. You are the Creator God who is always faithful in Your love and care; and these will endure forever. Even though most of the time, I don't fully get it.

Facilitated Prayer:

Find a location where you can focus your mind and calm your spirit as you move into a time of prayer. Spend the next few minutes using the P-R-A-Y prompts to enter into a conversation with God. The prompts are to help focus your time of prayer by taking the guesswork out of who and what to pray about each day.

·Day 64·

PRAY:

Praise	Take a minute to give thanks to the Lord for His steadfast and enduring love.
Repent	Take a minute to repent of times of unthankfulness.
Ask for Others	Take two minutes to pray for someone who needs to know the Creator of the universe.
Your Needs	Take two minutes to focus on God's faithfulness in His love and care for you!

Taking Notes:

_____

_____

_____

_____

_____

_____

_____

_____

_____

·Day 65·

Psalm 119:1-8
Justin Brinkmeyer | Edwardsville MetroGroup Leader

We all have something that acts as a wedge to make us think we aren't good enough. Sometimes we find ourselves believing the lie that our prayer doesn't matter since we have prayed so many times and asked God for help, and it seems He's not listening. We've all been there at some point in our faith journey. Maybe you are there now. God reminds us that he will not forsake His obedient children.

Often, the shame produced by our sin keeps us from connecting fully with God. Instead, the shame creates a wedge to make us think we aren't worthy or good enough to return to God. But really, the very thing that the evil one uses to drive us further away is the thing that God uses to pull us closer to him.

We gain freedom from shame through obedience to Him using His precepts in Scripture. Even in times of weakness, God wants to see our obedience to Him. He wants the posture of our hearts to align with His ways. When we fix our eyes on His commandments, we will not be put to shame.

Facilitated Prayer:

Find a location where you can focus your mind and calm your spirit as you move into a time of prayer. Spend the next few minutes using the P-R-A-Y prompts to enter into a conversation with God. The prompts are to help focus your time of prayer by taking the guesswork out of who and what to pray about each day.

·Day 65·

As you "P-R-A-Y..."

PRAY:

Praise	Take a minute to praise God for your ability to read and study His Word.
Repent	Take a minute to repent of times you have not diligently kept His Word, but leaned on your own understanding instead.
Ask for Others	Take two minutes to pray for friends and family who are caught up in the shame of sin and disobedience.
Your Needs	Take two minutes to commit to reading and obeying God's Word more diligently.

Taking Notes:

_____

_____

_____

_____

_____

_____

_____

_____

_____

·Day 66·

Psalm 119:9-16
Gavin McWhorter | Metro Outreach Director

I have never been a big reader. In fact, in grade school, I would make up my reading log entries when I hadn't done the reading because I just didn't enjoy reading and would rather use the effort doing something else. Now that I am older, I realize the reason I hated reading books was because I really didn't care about the story or didn't feel it had any value to me.

As I look at Psalm 119, I see that each verse of this psalm talks about the importance of reading God's Word. As a non-reader, this is difficult for me. But as I began to realize that my dislike for reading was due to apathy toward the subject, I began to realize that maybe I had an apathy toward God and who He is and that maybe that was causing me to not want to read His Word. I was living my life knowing who God is and what He did but not caring about the relationship He wanted with me.

Once I began to discover this about myself, I asked Him to transform me and give me a hunger for His Word so that I would care more about who He is and desire to have a real, personal relationship with Him. As I prayed this prayer, over time, I began to sense a change in my perspective; He had started working through me, ever so slowly, and I began to care more about Him and His ways. I found myself actually wanting to read His word, and even looking forward to when I could read His Word next.

These verses from Psalm 119 tell us to live our life according to His Word, seek Him with our whole heart, store His Word in our heart, learn His statues, meditate on His precepts, and delight in His statutes. These actions can only happen when we are reading His Word. If this is difficult for you, take it to God; ask Him to give you that desire. Because as you pray for these things and delve into His Word, He will provide you with a passion for His Word.

Facilitated Prayer:

Find a location where you can focus your mind and calm your spirit as you move into a time of prayer. Spend the next few minutes using the P-R-A-Y prompts to enter into a conversation with God. The prompts are to help focus your time of prayer by taking the guesswork out of who and what to pray about each day.

·Day 66·

PRAY:

Praise	Take a minute to praise God for the transforming power of His Word.
Repent	Take a minute to repent of any apathy you have toward reading the Bible.
Ask for Others	Take two minutes to pray for others who also struggle with having a passion for God's Word.
Your Needs	Take two minutes to commit to reading God's Word and to ask Him to give you a passion for Him and His Word.

Taking Notes:

_____

_____

_____

_____

_____

_____

_____

_____

Psalm 119:25-32
Connie Bolyard | Vandalia Metro Group Leader

In our life, if we are honest with ourselves, we have all hit rock bottom with no place to go. Maybe it was a time you sinned against God and continued to think you could handle the situation all by yourself. There are many ways we can hit rock bottom, but the good news is there is another way. Turn to God in prayer! Cry out to Hm.

Psalm 119:25-32 is an excellent Scripture to help when we hit rock bottom. I have hit rock bottom several times in my life. One time hit me harder than others. My dad and I have always been very close. He turned away from me. He even changed his phone number. The trouble was based on lies he had been told. It was totally Satan at work. I tried to do the "it's all good" thing which did not work. One day, I was home alone and I just couldn't take it anymore. I was depressed and weary down deep in my soul. I fell to the floor face down in my living room and cried out to God. I had a long conversation with God. I told Him everything that was on my heart and asked Him to make me whole again and strengthen me. I placed the situation with my dad into His hands. I asked God to help me understand and meditate on His wonders.

What became of that day? I went from desperation to dependence to devotion. In a nutshell. I was low in the dust, I prayed and was totally dependent on God. He turned this situation around and my dad came back to me. He even gave me his new phone number. I will continue being devoted to God. Prayer works! Devotion feels so much better than despair.

Facilitated Prayer:

Find a location where you can focus your mind and calm your spirit as you move into a time of prayer. Spend the next few minutes using the P-R-A-Y prompts to enter into a conversation with God. The prompts are to help focus your time of prayer by taking the guesswork out of who and what to pray about each day.

·Day 67·

PRAY:

Praise	Take a minute to praise God, that He is willing to meet us when we are in total desperation.
Repent	Take a minute to denounce any lies you have believed.
Ask for Others	Take two minutes to pray for those who need to have their heart "enlarged" so they can chase after God's will.
Your Needs	Take two minutes to pray to God about areas in your life that feel like you are on the verge of desperation.

Taking Notes:

_____

_____

_____

_____

_____

_____

_____

_____

Psalm 119:33-40
Ron Harris | Edwardsville Metro Group Leader

The Bible has a lot to say about what we are, who we are, and what kind of life we are supposed to live. Jesus gave us the perfect example of what that looks like, and I believe that most of us, if asked, would say yes to living that kind of life: a life pleasing to God. I would also say that most would agree that living this kind of God-pleasing life is good for us.

However, Psalm 119:33-40 is a reminder that following God is not always easy. There will be times when we are tempted to stray from His ways. There will be times when we fall, give in to our selfish human desires, put our own needs before the needs of others, and outright disobey God. Jesus understands this. He was tempted 'in all ways' as we are, yet did not sin. I can't imagine that was in any way easy for Him.

In Metro's DivorceCare, we talk a lot about forgiveness. As you can imagine, there are a lot of hard feelings in the light of divorce. Truth be told there generally isn't much interest, willingness, or desire to forgive after such deep hurt. What we teach in DivorceCare in regards to forgiveness is to ask God to help us get to a point where we are 'willing to be willing' (to forgive).

I believe this passage is leading us in that direction; the direction of His help. I don't know about you, but if I could do all of this myself, I would. If I could do what Jesus did when tempted, I would every time. But we can't. We NEED His help. We need Him to teach us, give us understanding, lead us, incline our hearts, turn our eyes. We need to ask for His help; and when we fall, we need His help getting up.

There's a verse that I try to recall when I struggle. It's Philippians 2:13, "for it is God who works in you, both to will and to work for his good pleasure" [ESV]. Oftentimes, we have the want, but not the will. Sometimes, we don't even have the want. If we truly desire to know and obey God, we must ask Him for His help. He WANTS to help us. He will give us the understanding and strength we need to follow Him.

Facilitated Prayer:

Find a location where you can focus your mind and calm your spirit as you move into a time of prayer. Spend the next few minutes using the P-R-A-Y prompts to enter into a conversation with God. The prompts are to help focus your time of prayer by taking the guesswork out of who and what to pray about each day.

·Day 68·

PRAY:

Praise	Take a minute to thank God for His willingness to help us through all of life's situations.
Repent	Take a minute to confess the times when you have the "the want, but not the will" to obey God.
Ask for Others	Take two minutes to pray for those who you know that need God's guidance for their life.
Your Needs	Take two minutes to ask for God's help with anything that is heavy on your heart.

Taking Notes:

_____

_____

_____

_____

_____

_____

_____

_____

·Day 69·

Psalm 119:57-64 | Sleepover with the Savior
Tim Wierauch | Vandalia Campus Pastor

Have you ever had a friend that you just had to spend time with? It didn't matter where it was. It didn't matter what you were going to do. You just wanted to be around each other. If you had the opportunity to have a sleepover with them, you may have even tried to stay up all night talking and enjoying each other's company. These kinds of relationships are special. Not everyone finds a friend like this, but we long for this; and when we find it, we often treasure it for as long as we possibly can.

This is the type of relationship described in this passage. We long to do what pleases the Lord (Yahweh). We pursue him with all of our heart. We change the course of our actions when we know it displeases Him. We long for others to know this great friend that we have. Even when we are losing sleep to build the relationship at all hours of the night, gratitude is the emotion within our hearts.

As you have been walking through this prayer journal, you have probably been awakened out of a dead sleep. Could it just be Jesus wanting to talk with you as a friend a bit more? Be willing to lose some sleep at the sleepover that Jesus has invited you to. Spend time in prayer sharing gratitude for what He is doing in your heart and those around you. Spend some time in prayer for those who have not found this Friend that you have. Ask God to draw them close to Him. Pray that they would respond to the love and instruction of the Best Friend they could ever navigate through life with.

Facilitated Prayer:

Find a location where you can focus your mind and calm your spirit as you move into a time of prayer. Spend the next few minutes using the P-R-A-Y prompts to enter into a conversation with God. The prompts are to help focus your time of prayer by taking the guesswork out of who and what to pray about each day.

·Day 69·

PRAY:

Praise	Take a minute to praise God for what He is doing in your heart.
Repent	Take a minute to repent of the times you have not given your relationship with Him priority in your life.
Ask for Others	Take two minutes to pray for those who have not found the Friend in Jesus that you have.
Your Needs	Take two minutes to ask God to continue to show you His truth and to help you to share it with others.

Taking Notes:

_____

_____

_____

_____

_____

_____

_____

_____

Psalm 119:73-80
Angel Creek | MetroGroup Leader

Do you search your heart before you act? We are all familiar with the adage "Those who are happiest are those who do the most for others." When we do something for others because we know in our hearts it is the right thing to do, it will affect the rest of our day, person, and life. Our hearts are the essence of who we are: our emotions, thoughts, motivation, courage, and actions. Knowing this, have you ever wondered how we know it is the right thing to do?

As Psalm 119 points out to us, God sought us out and put His principles in our hearts. As we examine our hearts and meditate on His Word, it provides the answers we need to navigate life. We seek by searching our hearts and praying; God provides through His established principles love, mercy, and grace.

When we search our hearts and pray about what we have found, we will want to trust and obey God. Living in this manner, we will seek out others who do the same. Together in community with other Believers, we will trust and obey God when He nudges or sometimes "body checks" us to action. Creating time for one another, worshiping together, and praying for all of our actions as a whole proves to be very powerful.

We seek answers, through prayer, so God uses our hearts to message us, so to speak. We thought we invented text messages but in all actuality God did. He sends His "text messages" via the Holy Spirit to our hearts to remind us of His principles. We know and understand (wisdom) these messages through our emotions, thoughts, motivation, courage, and actions which are influenced by His principles which we have meditated on. If we act or create a plan before we examine our hearts for God's text messages, we will often find that we make the wrong choices. However, when we funnel our actions through the truths in His Word and obey His principles, we find, as the psalmist says inf 119:80 that our "heart will be blameless" and we won't "be put to shame."

Facilitated Prayer:

Find a location where you can focus your mind and calm your spirit as you move into a time of prayer. Spend the next few minutes using the P-R-A-Y prompts to enter into a conversation with God. The prompts are to help focus your time of prayer by taking the guesswork out of who and what to pray about each day.

As you "P-R-A-Y..."

PRAY:

Praise	Take a minute to thank God for being your ultimate source of wisdom.
Repent	Take a minute to confess a time when you were arrogant and thought you knew better than God.
Ask for Others	Take two minutes to pray for those who need the infinite wisdom of God as they deal with difficult circumstances.
Your Needs	Take two minutes to seek God's wisdom (perspective) to assess your current circumstances.

Taking Notes:

_____

_____

_____

_____

_____

_____

_____

_____

_____

Psalm 119:97-104

Alyssa Liley | MetroCollege Leader

When we think of rules, there are usually two types of people: those who love them, and those who want nothing to do with them. But the author of Psalm 119 makes it clear that no matter which camp we fall into, God's rules are good and can be trusted.

The psalmist begins by stating that he loves God's law. In John 14:15, Jesus tells His disciples, "If you love me, you will keep my commandments." This teaches us it is our love for God that motivates us to strive towards obedience to His law. We must be careful not to let our love for the law become greater than our love for God - that would be idolatry and pushes us into legalism! Until our true motive is our genuine love for God, we will either follow His law for the wrong reasons, or we just won't follow it at all.

As we keep reading in this passage, we learn it is only through the wisdom revealed in God's law that we become aware of our missteps and our need to repent. The more we understand God's law, the more we see how often we fall short. As we let the Holy Spirit and God's Word reveal sinful patterns and habits in our lives, we must surrender, repent, and turn to follow God's instruction. Often, this feels more like a sting than sweet honey; but it is only through this act of surrender that we begin to see that a life aligned with God's law is sweeter than honey. God's Word is a blessing, and understanding it more deeply grows our love for God. As we live within the guidelines He gives us, we discover the abundant life He promises!

Facilitated Prayer:

Find a location where you can focus your mind and calm your spirit as you move into a time of prayer. Spend the next few minutes using the P-R-A-Y prompts to enter into a conversation with God. The prompts are to help focus your time of prayer by taking the guesswork out of who and what to pray about each day.

·Day 71·

PRAY:

Praise	Take a minute to thank God for His rules/laws that help us find abundant life in Him.
Repent	Take a minute to repent of any harbored sin in your life.
Ask for Others	Take two minutes to pray for those who are rebelling against God's laws. Pray that they seek God's forgiveness and want to follow Him.
Your Needs	Take two minutes to ask for God to lead and guide your life whenever you read His Word.

Taking Notes:

_____

_____

_____

_____

_____

_____

_____

_____

_____

·Day 72·

Psalm 119:97-104
Kim Casey | Vandalia MetroGroup Leader

"...I constantly take my life in my hands." Oh, how familiar I am to this verse! I take my troubles upon myself, into my own hands so many times. As a working Mom, I just take care of things as they come at me, multi-tasking and taking care of everyone, and that leads right into trying to take care of my entire life on my own. I think, "He has bigger problems to solve and people to perform miracles for." My stressful workday doesn't seem worthy to take to Him. This is so false! By not submitting ALL to Him, I am rejecting His opportunity to show me His miraculous power and love. He cares about ALL of my problems, no matter how big or small.

"I will not forget your law." I know that God is in control and His Word is written upon my heart. I never doubt Him or His plan for me and my life. We had a trial once when our youngest son had a fever for 21 days. As a nurse, I should have known it could mean cancer, but that had not even occurred to me until we went into the doctor's office late on a Friday afternoon, and he said, "Kim, you know this is serious." I was the busy mom who just wanted to get him to the doctor before the weekend. I was taking things into my own hands again. I remember taking him for a chest x-ray and bloodwork and feeling numb. I didn't have a problem praying then! On the way home, I made the mistake of looking at the report they placed in a brown envelope. The only reason they hand you an envelope is to take to your next appointment. I knew what this meant, so I told my husband to meet me at home and called my brother to come and pick up all of our boys. We got home and the doctor called to let us know he had arranged an appointment at Cardinal Glennon on Monday. He said to take a bag, because we might be there all week. After we had our moment of grief and feeling sorry for ourselves, we regrouped and were ready to take on whatever God had planned for us and our young son's life.

For those 2 days, I had fear, but also the biggest peace. I had followed a mom on Facebook who had just gone through this same experience. I knew that God had used this to prepare me for the battle we were about to face. I packed a bag and we had a plan for me to stay with him for however long I needed. My husband would return home and take care of our other two sons. We prayed and trusted God, and He blessed us with the biggest blessing. As a nurse, of course I had researched all weekend and came up with a possible, different diagnosis. And, we were miraculously blessed with the best news when the Cardinal Glennon oncologist told us that my diagnosis was exactly what he had. NOT cancer! The best words we could've possibly heard! Looking back, I see this was a test of our faith, and we were thankfully blessed and passed His test! Always keep God's promises and His Word in your heart. This is what you will need to cling to during those trying times. Come near to God and He will come near to you.

·Day 72·

Facilitated Prayer:

Find a location where you can focus your mind and calm your spirit as you move into a time of prayer. Spend the next few minutes using the P-R-A-Y prompts to enter into a conversation with God. The prompts are to help focus your time of prayer by taking the guesswork out of who and what to pray about each day.

As you "P-R-A-Y..."

PRAY:

Praise	Take a minute to thank God for opportunities for your faith to be tested.
Repent	Take a minute to release to God areas in your life that seem out of control.
Ask for Others	Take two minutes to pray for those you know in your life that need clear direction that only God's Word offers.
Your Needs	Take two minutes to pray that God's Word would help guide your decisions this week.

Taking Notes:

_____

_____

_____

_____

_____

Psalm 119:129-136
Kathy Pease | Edwardsville MetroGroup Leader

The faith journey is different for everyone. For some of us, it's a ride through mountaintops and then deep, even very deep, valleys. When we are high in the mountains, everything is good. We are optimistic, excited, and celebrating. In the deeper, darker valleys, we wonder if we even have the energy to climb back to the mountain tops.

This passage from the book of Psalms is titled "Pe," translated as "mouth". The words are almost a call or a prayer for a relationship with God: "I opened my mouth and panted: For I longed for your commandments." The verses ask God for grace, guidance, and strength. These are the very things we need during our journey. We only need to call out, using our voice (mouth), and ask for His presence in our lives.

Our roller coaster journey of life will always be there. We can hope for more mountains than valleys; and honestly, I would even be satisfied with a pleasant, even plain. Through the valleys and the mountaintops and even the plains, we need our relationship with God to sustain us. He provides grace when we neglect to nurture our relationship with him. He provides guidance as we navigate each day. He provides strength even when we get in our own way.

Have you used your "mouth" to call out to him today?

Facilitated Prayer:

Find a location where you can focus your mind and calm your spirit as you move into a time of prayer. Spend the next few minutes using the P-R-A-Y prompts to enter into a conversation with God. The prompts are to help focus your time of prayer by taking the guesswork out of who and what to pray about each day.

·Day 73·

PRAY:

Praise	Take a minute to call out to God and thank Him for His grace, guidance, and strength in your life.
Repent	Take a minute to reflect on a time when you remained silent instead of calling out to God.
Ask for Others	Take two minutes to pray for those who need God's help to guide them from the valleys to the mountains.
Your Needs	Take two minutes to open your mouth and ask God to help navigate the roller coaster of your life.

Taking Notes:

_____

_____

_____

_____

_____

_____

_____

_____

·Day 74·

Psalm 119:145-152
Penny Critcheloe | Vandalia MetroGroup Leader

I call with all my heart; answer me, Lord.

Have you ever found yourself whispering these words while on your knees or shouting them while angry or confused?

God tells us that He hears our prayers and answers our prayers. Prayer is to surrender to the will of God and cooperation with that will. To lay everything at His feet, to leave it there, and in return, feel peace that only God can give.

Have you ever felt Satan was attacking you or your family? Remember that Satan is only able to be in our lives momentarily and then he must move on.

Our God is Omnipresent. Constantly in our hearts. Always listening. He never leaves us! Psalm 119 reminds us that God's very character is reflected through His Word. He is Righteous, He is Faithful, He is Unchanging, He is True. We are blessed as we walk in His Truth and seek Him with our whole heart. To be a man or woman of God, you must be a man or woman of the Word. We can't know God apart from knowing His Word. We can't be devoted to God without devotion to His Word. We can't love God without loving His Word. We will go through trials in this life. To endure these trials, we need to be revived by His Word. We need God's Word as our light, so we are able to stay on His directed path.

Nothing on this earth compares to the value of God's Word. Hope in God's Word encourages us to continue in prayer. It is better to take time from sleep, than not find time for prayer. Let our Lord guard your heart by filtering emotions, desires, thoughts and responses through His Word. Begin your day in prayer and witness the peace that comes over you that only God can provide.

Facilitated Prayer:

Find a location where you can focus your mind and calm your spirit as you move into a time of prayer. Spend the next few minutes using the P-R-A-Y prompts to enter into a conversation with God. The prompts are to help focus your time of prayer by taking the guesswork out of who and what to pray about each day.

·Day 74·

PRAY:

Praise	Take a minute to praise God for always hearing your prayers.
Repent	Take a minute to repent for a lack of devotion to God's Word.
Ask for Others	Take two minutes to pray for someone who is struggling with prayer and surrender to the will of God.
Your Needs	Take two minutes to talk to God about how much time you are spending in His Word. Ask Him to guide you in committing to reading His Word more faithfully.

Taking Notes:

_____

_____

_____

_____

_____

_____

_____

_____

·Day 75·

Psalm 119:153-160
Jeff Loyet | Edwardsville MetroGroup Leader

As I begin this work week, I am reminded that God calls us to rest. Not just on the Sabbath but that we must allow ourselves to rest and recover. As a leader in my family, profession, and church family, I must remember to take the time to take care of myself. This is the type of example we should set for ourselves and others.

Being a leader, no matter the situation, will always open you to criticism. Being a leader and keeping a Christian attitude will increase these types of criticisms.

As a leader within our profession or workplace, we are constantly placed in scenarios where we must make decisions, that's why we're considered leaders. Not all of these decisions are faith based (i.e. assigning tasks within a project is not based on faith but probably skill) but the manner in which we carry ourselves or deliver these decisions can be. Do we treat others around the office with Godly respect as we interact with them? Do we treat our team members with Godly respect as we work with them on projects? Do we treat team members with Godly respect when we have to provide sometimes harsh criticism towards their work product? It's easy to be cruel or rude to make a point, so we must make sure we take the time to show compassion in this process. Perception is reality to others. If they perceive you to think a certain way because of your actions, then they might as well be right. If we are to live a Godly life living according to God's word and law, then we must ensure that we do this in all aspects. Living God's word and law at home but then ignoring God's word and law in other aspects of our lives is not okay. As Christians we must be able to do this in all aspects.

Facilitated Prayer:

Find a location where you can focus your mind and calm your spirit as you move into a time of prayer. Spend the next few minutes using the P-R-A-Y prompts to enter into a conversation with God. The prompts are to help focus your time of prayer by taking the guesswork out of who and what to pray about each day.

·Day 75·

PRAY:

Praise	Take a minute to praise God for opportunities to live out God's Word in front of others.
Repent	Take a minute to repent of times you brought criticism upon yourself because your actions and response to others did not line up with God's Word.
Ask for Others	Take two minutes to pray for broken relationships in your life. Ask God to give you opportunities to restore, ask forgiveness, and demonstrate a Christ-like love.
Your Needs	Take two minutes to pray that you represent God's Word and law as you interact with co-workers, neighbors, family, and friends today.

Taking Notes:

_____

_____

_____

_____

_____

_____

_____

_____

_____

Psalm 119:169-176
Ryan Heard | Edwardsville MetroGroup Leader

Psalm 119 is the longest chapter in the Bible. This very unique chapter forms an acrostic poem using the 22 letter Hebrew alphabet for each section with the 8 verses in each section beginning with that letter. Verses 169-176 fall under the last Hebrew letter, Taw. Being the last letter and last verses of this chapter, it makes me think of another ending more personal which is when I'm at my wit's end.

When you are at your wit's end, you are worried and tired due to a problem you cannot solve. You don't know what to do next. I have been in situations where I have tried to do things my way and yet became confused, perplexed, and agitated. Also, I have experienced painful circumstances that are not of my own doing which left me bewildered as to what to do next.

It is at these times we need to sincerely and humbly turn to God in prayer. God will always be there to listen to our cries, worries, and heartaches. Through the Bible, God has given us the blueprint or instructional manual for life. His commands, decrees, instructions, and regulations are there for our benefit. Even in the midst of life's challenges, His Word is righteous and worthy of praise.

By following God's commandments and combining it with the power of prayer, you can expect the Lord to provide wisdom to understand your next steps towards rescue from your difficult situation. The solutions and timing may not be what you had in mind or when you expected. I know this makes me feel uneasy because there may be new things I need to learn, old habits I need to break, or a delay when I want instant gratification. Yet, I also know God can do immeasurably more than I might ask or think; I only need to trust in Him. Praise God for his guidance, promises, and faithfulness!

Facilitated Prayer:

Find a location where you can focus your mind and calm your spirit as you move into a time of prayer. Spend the next few minutes using the P-R-A-Y prompts to enter into a conversation with God. The prompts are to help focus your time of prayer by taking the guesswork out of who and what to pray about each day.

As you "P-R-A-Y..."

PRAY:

Praise	Take a minute to thank God for providing us a "blueprint" for life through His Word.
Repent	Take a minute to repent of instant gratification that you seek that is apart from God and His Word.
Ask for Others	Take two minutes to pray for those who are at their wit's end and need God's wisdom to know their next steps.
Your Needs	Take two minutes to pray about anything in your life that is bewildering and ask God to make your next step clear through His Word.

Taking Notes:

_____

_____

_____

_____

_____

_____

_____

_____

·Day 77·

Psalm 121:1-8
Rachel Wierauch | Vandalia MetroGroup Leader

Have you ever had a fear or some sort of anxiety you didn't know how to describe? Recently, one of mine has been struggling to fall asleep. I don't know why this is happening, but I just don't want to fall asleep. Maybe it is because I don't want the day to end, maybe it is a fear of the unknown tomorrow that awaits, or maybe it is just the "what ifs" of what might happen in my sleep. I can never perfectly describe why I have anxiety related to falling asleep, but God knows. And He is always there.

The verses in this passage remind me that God never slumbers or sleeps. He is watching over my life in the day time and in the night time. I know anxiety doesn't just go away. Sometimes it is a lifelong battle, but I need to remember to keep praying to the One who is watching over me.

One of my children recently told me that they don't know what they will do when they leave for college, because I won't be there to keep them calm in times of their anxiety. Shouldn't we want that from God? To be in the constant presence of God through prayer? He is always there for us day and night. We can always take our worries and burdens to Him. Let him be the calm in your storm, the constant in your life.

Facilitated Prayer:

Find a location where you can focus your mind and calm your spirit as you move into a time of prayer. Spend the next few minutes using the P-R-A-Y prompts to enter into a conversation with God. The prompts are to help focus your time of prayer by taking the guesswork out of who and what to pray about each day.

·Day 77·

PRAY:

Praise	Take a minute to thank God because He offers rest to those whose minds are heavy laden.
Repent	Take a minute to trust the One who remains awake and alert so you can rest.
Ask for Others	Take two minutes to pray for those who need to know "God holds the high ground" and that they can find rest in Him.
Your Needs	Take two minutes to offer your worries and burdens to God so He can calm the storm in your life.

Taking Notes:

_____

_____

_____

_____

_____

_____

_____

_____

·Day 78·

Psalm 127:1-5
Tyler & Alexis Hasty | Edwardsville MetroGroup Leaders

It is often so easy for us to seek credit, control, and acknowledgement as we walk through this life. In general, life isn't easy. Hard work is earned, and anxiety comes with additional responsibility. Therefore, it is so easy for us to want to be the one on the podium collecting our trophy and returning home to the beaming eyes of our own family. At the end of the day, though, doesn't that become tiresome at some point? Sweating for the sake of our own repeated goals grows stale after a while, and stressing over the next day becomes wearisome.

This life can seemingly feel meaningless and worthless; however, it goes well beyond our own self-fulfillment, and it has no value for eternity if we do it without the Lord. This life is the Lord's. He is our builder, our protector, and our provider. Anything done apart from the Lord, even with the right intentions, is in vain. That's why it is so important that we simply put the Lord above all else. As today comes and goes, be still in His presence. Pause and talk to God. There are a hundred things to do and a thousand decisions to make. Each one can be fruitful or fruitless. Let Him simply lead the way. Resist your desire to take control. Allow Him to guide you as you work to build your house and family on the Lord. Let Him speak to you as you ground yourself in God's word. Allow yourself to be an instrument that God uses to apply Biblical principles within your family. Find rest in Him and let the results of today be a reflection of God's blessings.

His desires are beyond your greatest imagination, and He desires nothing more than your heart. He has equipped you for whatever is before you, and today is your opportunity to be the steward of God's gifts.

Facilitated Prayer:

Find a location where you can focus your mind and calm your spirit as you move into a time of prayer. Spend the next few minutes using the P-R-A-Y prompts to enter into a conversation with God. The prompts are to help focus your time of prayer by taking the guesswork out of who and what to pray about each day.

·Day 78·

PRAY:

Praise	Take a minute to thank God for equipping you for everything you will face today.
Repent	Take a minute to confess times you take too much credit and want to receive all the praises for life.
Ask for Others	Take two minutes to pray that God would use you as an instrument to impact those you care about.
Your Needs	Take two minutes to ask God for help in putting Him first in your life. Ask Him to reveal to you areas where you are investing time and energy that are worthless.

Taking Notes:

_____

_____

_____

_____

_____

_____

_____

_____

Psalm 128:1-6
Michelle Moore | Edwardsville MetroGroup Leader

When I accepted Jesus as my Lord and Savior as an adolescent, I remember praying that God would never take His Spirit from me. As I grew older and into adulthood, I remained involved in the church believing He was who He said He was and would do what He said He would do. However, into my early 50s, menopause, a neglected marriage, and an empty nest all came crashing onto me at the same time, and years of loneliness and vulnerability proved to be the perfect soil for the Enemy to step in. I came face to face with the Enemy, as he tempted me with thoughts of how much happier my life would be if I left my marriage. I wanted to believe him too, thinking that a change would give me happiness and peace.

Yet as I continued attending church every Sunday, God used sermons and songs to speak His Truth to my heart. His Spirit used many things and people to get my attention. I'm not exaggerating when I say that the battle for my soul was real. I knew what God's will for my life was, and it collided with my own; there was a battle going on inside of me. While I wanted to do His Will, I also found myself not wanting to stay in the marriage; I was chasing happiness.

Psalm 128 starts by saying that "Blessed (or Happy) is everyone who fears the Lord, who walks in his ways!" God requires obedience. I knew deep in my heart that I would not find happiness if I continued to run away from God's will in disobedience. His Spirit ruthlessly chased my spirit down; He never let me go, just as I had prayed when I first accepted Him into my life all those years ago. As a young girl, I had accepted His Lordship over my life; I believed then, as I believe now, that His plan for me and my marriage was perfect.

I came to a point where I stopped, obeyed, and trusted Him to repair and redeem my heart and my marriage. And He has and is doing all this and more as I walk in His ways, living a life of obedience. Obedience to God is the key that unlocks all the blessings God has for us.

Heavenly Father, we look to Jesus as the Perfect One who feared You and walked in Your ways. We long to do the same. Lord forgive us for the times we fall short of this. Teach us to fear You and walk in Your ways so that we may receive the blessings You have for us. In Jesus' mighty name, Amen

·Day 79·

Facilitated Prayer:

Find a location where you can focus your mind and calm your spirit as you move into a time of prayer. Spend the next few minutes using the P-R-A-Y prompts to enter into a conversation with God. The prompts are to help focus your time of prayer by taking the guesswork out of who and what to pray about each day.

As you "P-R-A-Y..."

PRAY:

Praise	Take a minute to thank God for equipping you for everything you will face today.
Repent	Take a minute to confess times you take too much credit and want to receive all the praises for life.
Ask for Others	Take two minutes to pray that God would use you as an instrument to impact those you care about.
Your Needs	Take two minutes to ask God for help in putting Him first in your life. Ask Him to reveal to you areas where you are investing time and energy that are worthless.

Taking Notes:

_____

_____

_____

_____

_____

_____

Psalm 130:1-8
Ryan Wedekind | Edwardsville MetroGroup Leader

Father, I am perpetually trapped in the abyss, and nothing that this world has to offer has proven sustainable. I can't see a glimpse of you, I can't hear you...but I know you hear me.

I recognize my hopelessness apart from you, Lord. You ordered the cosmos and delivered us from the chaos waters, but the distance between your glory and our realization is beyond my capability to traverse despite my best efforts.

Yet you say worthy...

With all our sins, worldly conventions, and convoluted priorities only ever proving a humanity bent towards walking away from you, still you have shown me enough; enough of your existence, enough of your unflappable character, enough of your unfailing grace.

Because of you, I can. Because of your Word, I will.

I serve with all I have but my stamina is guaranteed to give out with the weight of this world and my own selfishness. My flesh can't take it any longer! My eagerness for your kingdom to be fully realized in our lives is unrelenting and compounding with every minute that passes -to the point I'm reaching a singular focus of Jesus' return!

Alas, my hope in your rescue is as sure as the coming sun.

Brothers and Sisters, own your reality. Let us not be fooled or waste our energy seeking redemption, improvement, or even adequacy apart from God. Allow hope to fuel our patience, and believe in the One who hears. Trust in God's claim over us; we are His Love...incapable of losing it, and simply believing that truth will set us ALL free.

Facilitated Prayer:

Find a location where you can focus your mind and calm your spirit as you move into a time of prayer. Spend the next few minutes using the P-R-A-Y prompts to enter into a conversation with God. The prompts are to help focus your time of prayer by taking the guesswork out of who and what to pray about each day.

·Day 80·

As you "P-R-A-Y..."

PRAY:

Praise	Take a minute to praise God for the hope that He brings to your life.
Repent	Take a minute to confess and turn from your own selfishness.
Ask for Others	Take two minutes to think about and pray for opportunities for someone with whom you can share that true hope that only comes through Jesus.
Your Needs	Take two minutes to ask for help from God to put your trust and hope in Him through whatever hardships you are currently facing.

Taking Notes:

_____

_____

_____

_____

_____

_____

_____

_____

Psalm 134:1-3
Dennie Forehand | Vandalia MetroGroup Leader

I was raised in a very reserved church. I had no idea, until as an adult, that being expressive in my faith was okay with God! When I joined a new church and took a class to learn more about their beliefs, I remember telling the pastor, "I was raised in such & such way, and don't know that I will ever be comfortable raising my hands!" He confidently replied, "You will get there." Guess what? I did!

The hands are such a vital part of the fascinating bodies which God created. The hands are key indicators to our emotions as well. When we are worried or afraid, we often use them to hide our faces. When angry, we clench our fists; and when nervous, we may wring them together anxiously. Frustration causes us to throw them up in the air with impatience. At sporting events you will see us pumping our fists and raising them to cheer for the winning team! So when praising God, why would we NOT extend our hands up to the Heavens to express our love, our vulnerability, or our need for a Savior who can change situations over which we have little control?! It is our way of saying, "Here I am Lord, I come to You with open hands, holding nothing back." Our heart, soul, and body are all ONE when we raise our hands high toward heaven to declare His goodness.

I often reflect on a mental picture of the day I will meet Jesus face to face. On that day, will I feel "too reserved" or too embarrassed of what others may think about raising my hands in prayer & adoration at my homecoming? Of course not! So, if you are like I once was, give it a try as well. Raise those hands; it's a form of worship, prayer, gratitude, and thanksgiving!

He's waiting.

Facilitated Prayer:

Find a location where you can focus your mind and calm your spirit as you move into a time of prayer. Spend the next few minutes using the P-R-A-Y prompts to enter into a conversation with God. The prompts are to help focus your time of prayer by taking the guesswork out of who and what to pray about each day.

·Day 81·

PRAY:

Praise	Take a minute to think about why God is praiseworthy in your life right now.
Repent	Take a minute to seek if God would want you to meet with Him in worship in an intimate manner or just be a bystander.
Ask for Others	Take two minutes to pray for those who need to feel free to authentically express their heart of worship.
Your Needs	Take two minutes to ask God to help you prepare for worship. Pray about what it looks like to worship with your whole life and being.

Taking Notes:

_____

_____

_____

_____

_____

_____

_____

_____

Psalm 139:1-7
Darlene Tady | Edwardsville MetroGroup Leader

During my college years I spent a summer at a Christian Training Program in Colorado. It's the first time that I understood that God knew me perfectly and completely. Under the Colorado pine trees and deep blue skies my prayer went something like this: "LORD, you are the only one who knows me – my heart, my fears, my dreams, my strengths and weaknesses. I commit all these things into your capable and loving hands." I was enveloped by God's presence and peace as I cried out to him. In Psalms 139:1-6, David had a similar prayer time with God. He expressed to God three truths that were mind boggling to him (verse 6: "such knowledge is too wonderful for me, too lofty for me to attain.")

We can delight in these truths also:
God thoroughly knows us. Verse 1 says "You have searched me, LORD, and you know me." (NIV). Verses 2 and 3 show that He knows our daily activities, thoughts and tendencies. And verse 4 indicates that he even knows our unformed words, including our prayers, which He is busy answering before we speak; see Isaiah 65:24)

The word "know" used in these verses is the Hebrew word "yada" which includes but goes beyond an intellectual knowing to mean an intimate knowledge and decision to have a personal relationship. David is stating that the LORD chose to have a personal, intimate and covenant relationship with him even though He knew everything about David – the good, the bad and the ugly! This is the God we pray to – the One who knows us thoroughly! (He is omniscient.)

God's presence surrounds us. Verse 5 "You hem me in behind and before." (NIV)
Other translations shed further light: "You go before me and follow me." (NLT), "You are around me on every side." (GNT), "I look behind me and you're there, then up ahead and you're there too – your reassuring presence, coming and going." (MSG) This is the God we pray to – the One who surrounds us with His presence! (He is omnipresent)

God's strong hand is on us. Verse 5 "You lay your hand upon me." (NIV)
The Hebrew word for hand is "kap" and one of its meanings is "power." God is omnipotent or all powerful and His hand literally strengthens us. He "gives strength to the weary and increases the power of the weak...those who hope in the Lord will renew their strength." Isaiah 40:29, 31 (NIV) This is the God we pray to – the One who is all powerful! (He is omnipotent)

Psalm 139 is a song of praise to God. Praise Him for the reassuring truths that He knows you, surrounds you with His presence and strengthens you with his power.

·Day 82·

Facilitated Prayer:

Find a location where you can focus your mind and calm your spirit as you move into a time of prayer. Spend the next few minutes using the P-R-A-Y prompts to enter into a conversation with God. The prompts are to help focus your time of prayer by taking the guesswork out of who and what to pray about each day.

As you "P-R-A-Y..."

PRAY:

Praise	Take a minute to praise God for being all knowing, always presence, and all powerful!
Repent	Take a minute to give things over to God's "capable and loving hands" that you have been holding onto too tightly.
Ask for Others	Take two minutes to pray for someone who needs to know that God is aware of what they are going through. Pray for someone who needs to feel God's presence. Pray for someone else who needs God's strength to endure.
Your Needs	Take two minutes to ask God for help with whatever situations are heavy on your heart and mind.

Taking Notes:

_____

_____

_____

_____

_____

·Day 83·

Psalm 141:1-10

Erica Donoho | Edwardsville MetroGroup Leader

Who do you turn to when your car stops running? When your water pipes burst? When your computer crashes? You might answer, a mechanic, a plumber, a computer technician. We want someone with knowledge, an expert in their field. But who do you turn to when you are feeling drawn to sinful things?

When Jesus was in the flesh, he was tempted in every way and yet did not sin. He is the expert at defeating Satan and sin. Knowing that Jesus understands our struggles, we can confidently come to him for wisdom and strength to be victorious. We can trust that He will be our refuge, leading us safely through.

Hebrews 4:15-16 "For we do not have a high priest who is unable to empathize with our weakness, but we have one who has been tempted in every way, just as we are—yet he did not sin. Let us then approach God's throne of grace with confidence, so that we may receive mercy and find grace to help us in our time of need."

Walking through temptation and discipline can be painful or uncomfortable. We might decide it is too hard or too costly and give in to temptation. But God's wisdom is perfect, infinite, and for our good. He loves us and wants us to accept his help and find value in the training He provides. Proverbs 3:11-12 "My son, do not make light of the Lord's discipline, and do not lose heart when he rebukes you, because the Lord disciplines the one he loves, and he chastens everyone he accepts as his son."

Hebrews 12:7, 11 "Endure hardship as discipline; God is treating you as his children. For what children are not disciplined by their father? ...No discipline seems pleasant at the time, but painful. Later on, however, it produces a harvest of righteousness and peace for those who have been trained by it."

God has a bigger plan that is beyond our understanding. He can use our temptations to discipline us, to grow our character, to show us our weaknesses, and to glorify Himself. Our weakness is an opportunity to recognize His power to save us. Will you let Him be your refuge when you are overwhelmed in your struggle with sin?

·Day 83·

Facilitated Prayer:

Find a location where you can focus your mind and calm your spirit as you move into a time of prayer. Spend the next few minutes using the P-R-A-Y prompts to enter into a conversation with God. The prompts are to help focus your time of prayer by taking the guesswork out of who and what to pray about each day.

As you "P-R-A-Y..."

PRAY:

Praise	Take a minute to thank God for being your refuge when tempted.
Repent	Take a minute to turn to Jesus with sinful temptations you are feeling drawn to.
Ask for Others	Take two minutes to pray for those in your life that are struggling with addictions.
Your Needs	Take two minutes to pray over your own weakness and ask God for His strength to help you.

Taking Notes:

_____

_____

_____

_____

_____

Psalm 143:1-6

Eddie Lowry | Edwardsville MetroGroup Leader

That call that no one wants to receive. We were getting ready to attend a wedding and the phone rang. After a very brief introduction, an officer on the other end of the line stated that my in-laws were involved in a horrific car accident and both were being airlifted to a trauma center. My father-in-law was unlikely to survive. A day later he went home to be with Jesus.

The loss of a person that is that close to you causes a lot of despair. Our instinct was to pray, begging God for strength as the inevitable outcome of injuries to an 80 year old that most 20 year old people could not survive. The enemy stomps on you, buries you, weighs you down telling you that there is no hope, but then a light in the form of memories of him from those who came to the hospital and reminisced with our family shown through. These stories displayed his passion for people and showing them Jesus. My father-in-law bought Thanksgiving groceries for families that couldn't afford them. He befriended those who were freshly out of prison and needed a friend. He delivered Bibles worldwide to show the hope that only Jesus can bring.

We prayed and prayed over those few days asking God to please hear us. We prayed for Him to help us in our despair, but we also prayed thanking Him for the memories and the hope that one day we will be in His presence. In the end, we had tears of joy knowing that my father-in-law got to see Jesus. Jesus stretched out His hands and welcomed him home and I believe Jesus said, "Well done".

Through all the prayers, through all the pain and despair, God provided hope that one day we will be able see Jesus and He will welcome us home too.

Facilitated Prayer:

Find a location where you can focus your mind and calm your spirit as you move into a time of prayer. Spend the next few minutes using the P-R-A-Y prompts to enter into a conversation with God. The prompts are to help focus your time of prayer by taking the guesswork out of who and what to pray about each day.

·Day 84·

PRAY:

Praise	Take a minute to praise God for being a source of comfort.
Repent	Take a minute to admit times you have felt a situation is utterly hopeless.
Ask for Others	Take two minutes to pray for those in your life that have suffered a significant loss (job, spouse, death, miscarriage, etc.).
Your Needs	Take two minutes to call out to God where your spirit is faint. Ask Him to hear your prayers, and receive His mercy and grace.

Taking Notes:

_____

_____

_____

_____

_____

_____

_____

_____

Psalm 143:7-12
BJ & Melissa Deal | Vandalia MetroGroup Leaders

Have you ever felt so deeply troubled that your mind plays tricks on you, causing you to think God has turned His face from you? In those moments your prayers can feel a bit like they are not being heard, let alone answered.

In this passage, King David reminds us we are not alone in these thoughts. In the midst of being a fugitive, this great King was significantly troubled with threats on his life, and dysfunction from his very family. God are you there? Do you hear me, Lord? He seeks him in the morning and the evening. He seems to beg God for a quick answer of encouragement and wisdom of what to do next in this time of trouble. He was pleading with the Lord for a glimpse of His goodness while reminding Him of His righteousness and attributes. The emotions are so thick in this Psalm, that they almost have tangible weight.

So, when you have troubles weighing on you, what do you do, where do you turn? Do you close your eyes and worry? Do you hunker under the doubts, or do run to the shelter of His lovingkindness?

David reminds us that our prayers do not have to be tidy and proper. They can and should be broken, raw, and honest. After humbly pouring out our hurts, worries, and doubts, we can leave His presence with a different perspective. Perhaps not an answer, but a reminder and assurance of who He is and what He is fully capable of. This kind of praying can drastically change us.

Facilitated Prayer:

Find a location where you can focus your mind and calm your spirit as you move into a time of prayer. Spend the next few minutes using the P-R-A-Y prompts to enter into a conversation with God. The prompts are to help focus your time of prayer by taking the guesswork out of who and what to pray about each day.

·Day 85·

PRAY:

Praise	Take a minute to praise Him for being a God who listens.
Repent	Take a minute to admit times you felt God has "turned His face from you."
Ask for Others	Take two minutes to pray for those in your life who have troubles that are weighing them down.
Your Needs	Take two minutes to ask God to give you a different perspective that He wants you to see.

Taking Notes:

_____

_____

_____

_____

_____

_____

_____

_____

·Day 86·

Psalm 144:1-8
Mati Barron | Metro Communications Team

Have you ever been handed a task or responsibility that you were completely under trained for? Some people thrive and rise to the occasion, others of us struggle with feeling unprepared or supported in our tasks. It's not a great feeling – like you've been thrown into chaos with no direction, getting a thumbs up and a "you'll do fine!", and being left to figure it out for yourself!

In moments of high pressure, relational tension, or navigating new and uncharted territory, sometimes we can start to feel like God has sort of left us to struggle it out on our own. When we're in the midst of a battle, it's easy as humans to see our lack of comfort or control as a sure fire sign that we have been stranded by God when we needed Him most! Despite our best efforts to effectively handle our situations, we still find ourselves overwhelmed.

Psalm 144:1 speaks to the nature of God as we navigate the battlefield of life. Not only does He deliver us from battles, but it says He also trains our hands and fingers to fight alongside Him. He is our love and our fortress when we need protection from the blows of the enemy. He is our stronghold and shield when we need to rest after fighting a while. The Lord doesn't abandon us to figure it out alone, He loves us enough to prepare us to take on the challenges the enemy will throw our way.

If you're feeling like you're standing alone in the middle of the battlefield right now, it's time to claim the promises God has made us in His Word. He doesn't promise us an easy life, but He promises to provide unshakable love, guidance, power, and to work everything for His glory and our good.

 If you're in need of a battle cry today, continue to pray this scripture:

Blessed be the Lord, my rock, who trains my hands for war, and my fingers for battle; he is my steadfast love and my fortress, my stronghold and my deliverer, my shield and he in whom I take refuge, who subdues peoples under me."
Psalm 144:1-2

Facilitated Prayer:

Find a location where you can focus your mind and calm your spirit as you move into a time of prayer. Spend the next few minutes using the P-R-A-Y prompts to enter into a conversation with God. The prompts are to help focus your time of prayer by taking the guesswork out of who and what to pray about each day.

·Day 86·

PRAY:

Praise	Take a minute to thank God for being with you during life's battles.
Repent	Take a minute to confess times you have felt left alone by God in your struggles.
Ask for Others	Take two minutes to pray for your friends that need to experience God as their rock during a challenging time.
Your Needs	Take two minutes to ask Him to fight your battles and be your deliverer.

Taking Notes:

_____

_____

_____

_____

_____

_____

_____

_____

Psalm 145:1-9 | Truth in Praise
Scott Moore | Edwardsville MetroGroup Leader

Have you ever met someone who could not stop talking about himself? Rather than a dialogue, every conversation turns into a monologue. Can anything be worse than "those" people? Or how about a child who can only say "no" and ask for things? And just when I start to feel good about myself in comparison, I am reminded how often I do just that to the God of the Universe – talking at Him, telling Him what I want and need and where my "boundaries" are.

Simply put, prayer is communication with God. And though we are encouraged to make our requests known to Him, my sense is that my requests and talking about me is probably the lowest form of prayer. What might be the highest? How about praises about Him? Psalm 145 reads like a greatest hits listing of his praiseworthy qualities. He is inscrutably great and majestic. He is gracious, full of compassion, and merciful. It's easy to just read over those words. It is better to meditate on them ("whatever is true . . . think about such things." Philippians 4:8). In a world where truth is hard to find and often mocked, this Psalm declares truths that should form the bedrock of our understanding of and relationship with God. And as I ponder these truths concerning His majesty and goodness, they cannot help but pass from my head to my heart.

Have you ever said something ugly and then wondered "where did that come from"? The unfortunate truth is that, per Jesus, "out of the overflow of the heart, the mouth speaks." The flip side is that once God's praiseworthy qualities find their way into my heart, the overflow will start to sound like the psalmist David here, extolling my God and king.

Should this heart attitude be something I do or something I need to simply be. The answer is "yes." The more time I spend meditating on and praising God, the more automatic and deeper my meditations and praises will become.

And finally, how should I communicate these prayers of praise? Spoken words are fine, but most psalms were originally put to music, and songs have a unique way of drawing out deeper emotions and being more memorable at the same time. So, in the lyrical style of Michael W. Smith:

> Great is the Lord,
> And worthy of glory,
> Great is the Lord,
> And worthy of praise!
> Great are you Lord!

Facilitated Prayer:

Find a location where you can focus your mind and calm your spirit as you move into a time of prayer. Spend the next few minutes using the P-R-A-Y prompts to enter into a conversation with God. The prompts are to help focus your time of prayer by taking the guesswork out of who and what to pray about each day.

As you "P-R-A-Y..."

PRAY:

Praise	Take a minute to praise God for His majesty!
Repent	Take a minute to confess times when you used prayer as the sole means to telling God what you want.
Ask for Others	Take two minutes to ask God to display His compassion and mercy for those who do not know Him.
Your Needs	Take two minutes to meditate on God's goodness. Tell God how He has radically changed your life and how He is deserving of all your praise.

Taking Notes:

_____

_____

_____

_____

_____

Psalm 145:10-21
Marcus Barnes | Campus Worship Leader

If you take a look at everything God has done or created, they can't help but point to Him. From the way nature reflects his beauty, to when He heals or saves someone, it leads to His name being glorified. All of his works glorify Him and lead others to encounter Him and experience His faithfulness.

God keeps his promises and one of these being that He will never leave or forsake us. I think often when we walk through seasons of life that are difficult, we begin to believe that God's not with us in those times, but actually He wants to be closer to us and bring us comfort and peace. He wants us to call on Him and invite Him into our mess, not distance ourselves from Him in the storm. I know none of us want to walk through difficult seasons; but I do try to have the perspective since they are inevitable, that if it wasn't for the hard seasons, I wouldn't get to experience God's character of being there with me and being my comfort and peace in the midst of struggle.

So I may not necessarily ask God to let me go through difficult seasons because I'd definitely be okay to not walk through pain and what not, but I am thankful that God is there with me and doesn't leave me all alone in those times. For me, sometimes it's still easier said than done, but I know I need to remember to call on Him in prayer when I find myself walking through situations that don't look how I'd like them to look. I need to continually trust and remind myself that He's in control, He's faithful, and He won't ever fail or forsake me. He hears my prayers when I call and He is faithful to answer according to His perfect will.

Facilitated Prayer:

Find a location where you can focus your mind and calm your spirit as you move into a time of prayer. Spend the next few minutes using the P-R-A-Y prompts to enter into a conversation with God. The prompts are to help focus your time of prayer by taking the guesswork out of who and what to pray about each day.

·Day 88·

PRAY:

Praise	Take a minute to thank God for being with you during difficult seasons.
Repent	Take a minute to admit times you have distanced yourself from God.
Ask for Others	Take two minutes to pray for those you love going through a difficult season. Pray that they feel God's nearness to them.
Your Needs	Take two minutes to help you walk through any difficulties that you are currently facing.

Taking Notes:

_____

_____

_____

_____

_____

_____

_____

_____

_____

Psalm 148:1-14
Travis Bowman | Metro Worship Director

I find this Psalm incredibly challenging, not because it's anything difficult to read or because it's particularly convicting, but because it reminds me how incredibly expansive God is and how finite my worship of Him can be.

I love singing and using the gift of music that God gave us to worship Him. So much so that sometimes it becomes the only way that I worship Him throughout the week. Sunday morning I find myself walking into church without having spent any time praising my amazingly worthy God. How prideful of me to think that 1 hour a week out of 168 possible hours is enough to truly praise God!

See the Psalmist covers a very interesting list of what worships God. Did you catch it? The Heavens and the Earth, the sun, or maybe better termed our light source, the stars, the sea creatures, the land itself, the land animals, the birds of the sky, and finally man. Does that list maybe sound a little familiar to you? It should because this is the same list as the days of creation.

The Bible tells us that everything in all of creation cries out to worship God; not because He made it or sustains it, but because He is powerful. He is awe inspiring. He is loving. He is good. He is kind. And He is worthy. Our God has proven time and time again that He is worthy of our praise, and not just one hour a week when we walk through those big glass doors on Sunday. But every hour of our existence. Let the name of the Lord be praised in my life, in the life of our church, in the life of each individual reading this, in our families, in our children, in our alone time, in our friendships, in our jobs, in our cars.

In everything that we do, with everything that we have, praise the name of the Lord.

·Day 89·

Facilitated Prayer:

Find a location where you can focus your mind and calm your spirit as you move into a time of prayer. Spend the next few minutes using the P-R-A-Y prompts to enter into a conversation with God. The prompts are to help focus your time of prayer by taking the guesswork out of who and what to pray about each day.

As you "P-R-A-Y..."

PRAY:

Praise	Take a minute to praise God wherever you are at or whatever you are doing!
Repent	Take a minute to confess times you have limited your worship of God to one hour a week during church services.
Ask for Others	Take two minutes to pray for your neighbors and coworkers to come to know Jesus as their Lord and Savior, resulting in praise to Him.
Your Needs	Take two minutes to pray about how you can incorporate praising Jesus throughout your whole day.

Taking Notes:

_____

_____

_____

_____

_____

Psalm 150:1-6
Lindsey Bowman | Metro Worship Leader

This last Psalm of the Bible wraps together the foundation of a prayer through worship answering some grounding questions: where we pray, why we pray, how we pray and who can pray. This psalm focuses on praise, which is joyous prayer in worship to God. Let's learn about the answers to the foundational questions from above, while also applying praise in each circumstance.

Psalm 150:1- Where: we can praise God anywhere.
God's praise comes from us (we are His sanctuary) and He can be praised anywhere the sky surrounds, which means we can praise Him anywhere. Lift a prayer of praise to God wherever you are, thanking Him for being able to give Him praise and pray to him wherever we are.

Psalm 150:2- Why: The reasons we praise God
If you've read this far into this guide for prayer, you definitely have experienced some mighty works God has done in and around you. He is to be praised for the things He has done! Pause and thank God, recalling the things He has done in your life and in the lives of others you are close to.
As we recognize the things God has done, let us not forget the most important reason why we praise Him: because He is excellent in His own greatness. There is no one better than God. There is no one greater than God. He shows us just how important connecting with imperfect people is while being perfect, and there is no one or no thing better in all of the universe. This should draw out shouts of praise to Him. Pray thankfully to God for being most excellent in Himself, while also making a way in Jesus for us to have a relationship with Him.

Psalm 150:3-5- How we praise God.
We see all the items used to praise God in this psalm indicating the use of instruments (yes, even "the dance" is actually translated as an instrument in this passage). However, all the instruments have different functions of praise. You don't have to be musically inclined to praise the Lord. I do want to give you a picture of why so many instruments are listed and what their functions are, as we learn that praise has different functions:
-The trumpet gives a majestic or declarative tone when played, used to praise God for His majesty.
-The lute and harp, as well as stringed instruments later in the passage, share a peaceful reverence in praise.
-The timbrel, like a drum, is used to evoke a grounded, louder form of praise.
-The dance, translated as a pipe, sounds new melodies of praise to God. Flutes also give a similar sound which can give endless melodies of praise.
-Loud and clashing cymbals are used somewhat like shouts in music. God is pleased when we shout our praises to Him!

Made in the USA
Monee, IL
18 September 2023

42926033R00103